FLAVOURS OF DELHI

A Food Lover's Guide

Charmaine O'Brien

PENGUIN BOOKS

PENGUIN BOOKS

Published by the Penguin Group

Penguin Books India Pvt. Ltd, 11 Community Centre, Panchsheel Park, New Delhi 110 017, India

Penguin Group (USA) Inc., 375 Hudson Street, New York, New York 10014, USA

Penguin Group (Canada), 90 Eglinton Avenue East, Suite 700, Toronto, Ontario, M4P 2Y3, Canada (a division of Pearson Penguin Canada Inc.)

Penguin Books Ltd, 80 Strand, London WC2R 0RL, England

Penguin Ireland, 25 St Stephen's Green, Dublin 2, Ireland (a division of Penguin Books Ltd)

Penguin Group (Australia), 250 Camberwell Road, Camberwell, Victoria 3124, Australia (a division of Pearson Australia Group Pty Ltd)

Penguin Group (NZ), cnr Airborne and Rosedale Roads, Albany, Auckland 1310, New Zealand (a division of Pearson New Zealand Ltd)

Penguin Group (South Africa) (Pty) Ltd, 24 Sturdee Avenue, Rosebank, Johannesburg 2196, South Africa

Penguin Books Ltd, Registered Offices: 80 Strand, London WC2R 0RL, England

First published by Penguin Books India 2003

Text copyright © Charmaine O'Brien 2003
Photographs copyright © Kirsten Grant 2003

All rights reserved

10 9 8 7 6 5 4

Typeset in AGaramond by Eleven Arts, New Delhi
Printed at Saurabh Printers Pvt. Ltd, New Delhi

Contents

Contents

Acknowledgements

My sincere thanks and affection to Kinny and Gogi Sandhu, Amrita and Ranjit Batra, Bhuvan Kumari and Mr and Mrs D. Majithia—without your warm company and generous hospitality I do not think I would have come to know and love Delhi (and India) as I do.

For assistance with research in Delhi I would like to thank Mr Aleemuddin at Karim's, Mr Kishan Chander Yadav and Mr Sohan Bindroo at Hyatt Regency, Mr Narenjan at Sagar, Dhanji Cook at Suruchi, Chef Ashaque at Maurya Sheraton, Priti Narain, and Roop Chakravorty for chauffering me around.

Thank you also to Jo Swiney, Sonie Wilson and Matt Willamson for reading chapter drafts and offering considered advice; to Kirsten Grant for her patience and creativity in taking the photographs for this book and V.K. Karthika and Diya Kar Hazra at Penguin India for their support and feedback.

Introduction

■ *The Book*

My aim in writing this book is to give the reader a complete picture of the food life in the city of Delhi. Beginning with a comprehensive exploration of the city's culinary history, the book winds up in the fashionable cafés and restaurants of modern Delhi. I have tried to make history come alive by including recipes old and new, that will allow the reader to recreate the flavours of the city in his or her home. The latter half of the book is more akin to a restaurant guide and includes a guide to food shopping in Delhi. I have not offered a comprehensive list of restaurants (there are thousands in the city), instead I have chosen to focus on the places that offer the best examples of the style of food I am writing about. I have also directed the reader to a broad range of eating places as my intention is to guide him or her to the best food and this does not always mean the most expensive. My choices range from spartan dhabas to seriously expensive hotels. The difference between these places is often not the food but the surroundings. A simple rule of thumb to follow: if I have recommended a restaurant in a hotel—and many of Delhi's best restaurants are in five-star hotels—then you can be assured that it is expensive. Most other restaurants are reasonable and dhabas, sweet shops and street stalls are inexpensive.

In the past five years or so Delhi has experienced a boom in dining out and the number of eating places has proliferated at a great rate. As in many cities around the world, it has become very fashionable in Delhi to have an interest in a restaurant. While many novice restaurateurs may have great ideas and be serving up good food, they may not have the stamina or business acumen that it requires to ensure longevity in the restaurant game. Consequently places can come and go; often very quickly. I have done my best to ensure that all information in this book is correct at the time of printing but it may be prudent to call and check the current operating details and status of any of the places recommended.

I have also included some suggested tours for those readers who would like to both see and 'taste' the city. I do not expect that the reader will be limited to the suggestions that I have made in the book but that the information I have provided will encourage the reader to his or her own explorations.

■ *Delhi*

The first time I landed in Delhi was 23 November 1995. I spent a few days in the city; I did not like it. I had come to India to see all the magical places I had heard about— Varanasi, Rajasthan, Rishikesh, Khajuraho, the Taj Mahal. The country I wanted to see was tourist brochure India: dusky women in jewel-coloured saris gliding through beautiful stark desert landscapes; hawk-eyed men in ice-cream-coloured turbans and big gold earrings; marble palaces glimmering pink in the early morning light; decorated elephants; snake charmers; fortune tellers. Nothing had prepared me for the capital of India.

Delhi was obtrusive—the mass of people; the vehicles moving madly across intersections; the unrelenting bleating of car horns; the stinking public urinals and everywhere men spitting out streams of blood-coloured liquid. Delhi was polluted; it was not magical in the least. I bought a train ticket to Agra and left. I had no idea as I headed off to see the Taj Mahal that the man who built this famous monument had also created a marvellous city in Delhi.

28 November 1996, I was back in Delhi again. A friend's wedding celebrations necessitated that I spend two weeks in the city. This time the damp smell of Indira Gandhi Airport seemed familiar and welcoming. I was better prepared for Delhi this time. I had shed my travel

brochure notions and was ready for the shoe-shinewallahs in Connaught Place.

I saw a bit more of Delhi and begrudgingly began to like it. I discovered Old Delhi and some of the city's culinary treasures. I ate Mughlai food, plenty of tandoori food and I threw caution to the wind and started eating from promising-looking street stalls (I did not get sick from this and remain convinced that some of the best food in Delhi can be had from these stalls).

I was still blissfully ignorant though, of what a city this had once been. As soon as the wedding festivities were over I left Delhi to see and taste more of India.

My travels in India had introduced me to the incredible diversity of cuisine eaten throughout the country. I was astounded at how little we really know of Indian food in the West. All the Indian restaurants I had been to at home served the same dishes. I thought that palak paneer, roghan josh, aloo dum, dal, garlic naan and tandoori chicken *were* Indian food. How exciting it was to find out otherwise!

It was obvious that changes in geography and climate influenced culinary differences throughout India but there were so many other variables that had determined what people ate. The food of each region, community, or class of people told a story; their histories were captured in their food. I had become besotted with India and wanted to know more. What better way to learn about this incredible country than through her food! My millennium year resolution was to write a book about food in India.

March 2000. I had packed up my life in Australia to come to India to write my book on Indian food. I knew I wanted to write about food in India, but which food, where and how and when? I decided to make a start in Delhi. I began exploring food markets and visiting restaurants but the searing summer heat eventually drove me out of the city.

I escaped to the mountains where friends provided generous refuge and a copy of *City of Djinns: A Year in Delhi* by William Dalrymple. The book properly introduced me to a city that I realized I had not been giving due consideration to. I had an 'Eureka' moment—the story of the food of Delhi was going to be my book. I came down from the mountains and began my own 'year of living in Delhi'.

Delhi has been the capital of India only for the last ninety-two years but she has long been an important city. Situated at the point where the Aravalli Ranges taper off and meet the right bank of the Yamuna river, this geographic configuration creates a natural funnel for traffic into central and southern India. The obvious strategic advantages of holding such a position made Delhi a magnet for invaders. From early in history it has been said that 'he who holds Delhi holds India'.

Successive invaders undertook expensive expeditions, travelling thousands of kilometres on horseback to try their hand at conquering, plundering and ruling Delhi. What a fantastic city Delhi must have been to keep attracting such attention and to keep rising from the ashes (often literally) of each invasion.

The most obvious legacy of Delhi's past is in the architecture of the city. The buildings of Delhi's *Mahabharata* era only live on in legend but each subsequent ruler, from the seventh-century Rajput kings to the British Raj, contributed to Delhi's rich architectural history. Walk or drive anywhere in Delhi and you will see the remains of earlier cities: ancient domes hover over new homes; crumbling walls of older cities mark the boundaries of modern suburbs; green parks are dotted with ancient mosques and decaying forts; a traffic roundabout is built around a medieval tomb. Typically those who want to learn about Delhi study the architecture of the city, but another way to learn about Delhi is through her food. Everybody who has come here has eaten. Just as each ruler left their architectural mark on the city, so each bequeathed to the city a culinary legacy.

One

∎

ANCIENT DELHI: hindu roots

Every city has a beginning, and the chronological starting point most often cited for Delhi is around 1450 BC. It was at this time that the seminal city of Delhi, Indraprastha, is said to have been established on the right bank of the Yamuna. Available literary 'historical' references describe Indraprastha as a city of gleaming white buildings and pavilions set upon broad, well-planned streets marked at intervals with spectacular water tanks, ponds, lakes and pleasure hillocks. Most prominent amongst the city's buildings and manicured gardens was a golden-pillared hall studded with precious stones; at its centre there was an immense lotus pond of such exquisite clarity as to appear like glass. The epithet 'the admiration of the world' does not seem immoderate for such a city. The timely services of the 'voracious fire god, Agni' had also cleared the dense forests around Indraprastha making the land suitable for agriculture.

The source of this splendid vision of Indraprastha, the *Mahabharata*, is one of the great epics of India. Its central story concerns the civil war waged between the Pandavas and their cousins, the Kauravas, for control over the kingdom of Kurukshetra, which included the area of Delhi. Unlike modern historians, the ancient Indians were not particularly concerned with recording 'facts' about their lives. Instead they wove them into magical and expansive religious and philosophical works. The purpose of these works was intended to be allegorical (the *Mahabharata* teaches the concept of dharma or spiritual righteousness and well-being) yet the preference of the chroniclers of ancient India for promulgating and recording fables over setting down scientific and civic observations has meant that these mythological works have often had to suffice as sources of history. The history of ancient Delhi is no exception.

Archaeological discoveries have shown that Delhi is an ancient city but sadly, they do not support the popular birthdate of Delhi or the majestic description of Indraprastha found in the *Mahabharata*. There is no material evidence of human habitation in Delhi circa 1450 BC but pottery shards and other artefacts unearthed at the Indraprastha site (the Purana Qila area) indicate habitation of the area at around 1000 BC. These findings also quash the notion that a city existed on this site around 1000 BC; cities in fact did not exist anywhere in India at that time.[1] The most feasible picture of Indraprastha is

---

[1]There had been cities in the Indus Valley previous to this but

that of a village with its inhabitants dwelling in compact huts constructed of earth, wooden poles and sticks—hardly the gleaming white edifices that the *Mahabharata* describes! There is also supporting evidence that the impenetrable forests that once covered the Delhi area were 'devoured' by fire but the absence of iron tools in 1000 BC meant that burning on such a large scale was the only method available to clear such dense growth.

And what of the people who cleared these forests? And who, whether dwelling in city or village, were the pioneers of Delhi and, most importantly for our purposes, what did they eat?

Delhi's first inhabitants were the people historically referred to as Aryans. The Aryans came to India from Central Asia around 1500 BC[2]. Traditionally a semi-nomadic race, their lives were shaped by the seasons and the needs of the cattle and other animals that they herded. Changing climatic conditions and competition for territory

---

these cities had long disappeared by 1000 BC. This will be discussed later in this chapter.

[2]This is the accepted view of early Indian history but it is contentious. Opposing views argue that the Aryans were actually the people of the Harappan civilization and that the effects of devastating floods drove them out of India into Iran and surrounding countries. There is also argument over the use and meaning of the term 'Aryan'. I am taking the well-worn route here because the whole issue is much bigger than this little book.

pushed them out of the grasslands of the Central Asian
steppe through the Hindukush and into the Indus Valley.
Here they encountered the decline of a thousand-year-
old (Harappan) civilization that had existed in a network
of highly developed urban settlements along the banks
of the valley's rivers. There is no historical clarity as to the
interactions between the Aryans and the Harappans, but
it seems this encounter caused the Aryans to do two things:
create a caste system and modify their itinerant way of life.

The Aryans were a fair-skinned people and the
Harappans quite dark. Not wanting to mix with the locals,
the Aryans designated themselves as 'high' caste and the
darker Harappans as 'low' caste. Inevitably, the two tribes
intermingled and as Aryan society developed, new divisions
were required into which to fit people. Thus evolved the
caste system of India.[3] This caste system and the spiritual
beliefs, philosophies and practices of the Aryans eventually
became the religious and social system that we now call
Hinduism.

Although the Aryans adopted a settled pattern of living
in India, they were not interested in the urban existence
the Harappans had developed and preferred to live in small
self-contained rural villages. (This preference for rural
life still dominates India today; despite her bulging cities,

---

[3] This is a very simplified description of the evolution of something
as complicated as the Hindu caste system.

the majority of India's population still live in villages and engage in agricultural occupations.) The Aryans may have been determined to distance themselves from the local inhabitants both by caste and lifestyle but they were not adverse to gathering practical and theoretical knowledge from them.[4]

When the Aryans entered India their diet would have been a simple one that predominantly comprised *milk* and *meat*. From the Harappans they learnt how to enhance their diet with indigenous flavours—fenugreek, pepper, cardamom, mustard, ginger and turmeric—and how to grind spices using a mortar and pestle.

The central focus of the Harappan civilization and diet were cultivated crops such as *barley*, *millet*, *wheat* and *legumes*. These were ground using stone grinders into smaller fragments and flours and then used to produce a variety of cooked items such as *flat breads*, *gruels* and *fried cakes* (like a patty or rissole). The constant movement of their previous existence had not allowed the Aryans to cultivate crops, but once settled in India, they soon became adept at raising and preparing cereal foods. They also learnt from the Harappans how to extract oil from seeds such as sesame and mustard, and soon developed a passion for little cakes of ground barley, legumes or wheat fried in oil

---

[4]It is likely that the Aryan culture subsumed the remnants of the Harappan one.

and sprinkled with *ghee* and *honey*. Ghee was something the Aryans may have already been familiar with, but the flat metal plates that they cooked these cakes on and the methods used to extract honey were appropriated from the Harappans. One of Delhi's most ancient tastes are the little cakes of split peas fried by street vendors and served smothered with curd and sweet-and-sour mango or tamarind chutney.[5]

Not only did the Aryans gather their methods of cooking from the Harappans, they also borrowed the shape of their cooking pots and utensils from them. The *degchi*, *tava*, *kadhai*, spouted water pots and flat stone and cylindrical stone roller used for grinding spices and chutneys that have been for millennia—and remain—the basic items of the Indian kitchen, all had their genesis in the Harappan kitchen. Indeed the shapes of these vessels have changed little over time.

India also provided the Aryans with an abundance of native fruit and vegetables: pumpkin, varieties of gourd, cucumber, leafy green vegetables, radish, ginger, watermelon, pomegranate, banana, plantain, citrus fruit, roseapple, jackfruit, mango and tamarind. It was from this abun-

---

[5]Today these 'cakes' are more commonly available made with potato. Technically speaking this is not an 'ancient' taste as the potato did not come into India until the eighteenth century, but the method and form are ancient.

dance that the diverse cuisine of the Aryan/Hindu grew.

The Aryans initially settled in the Punjab. As their numbers grew, they gradually began to push out across the Gangetic valley clearing the heavy indigenous forests, and settling villages such as Indraprastha. Even as the Aryans extended their dominion over thousands of kilometres, they maintained a highly uniform pattern of living. As we have little direct record of what the Aryan inhabitants of Indraprastha were eating, we can assume that their diet was also subject to this conformity; what was eaten in Indraprastha would have been almost identical to what their brethren were eating across northern India.

The Harappans were familiar with *rice* but it was only cultivated on the eastern-most tip of their territory where the rainfall was sufficient to allow its cultivation. The Aryans had forged much of their territory across the lush Gangetic plain and the climatic conditions prevailing there made it ideal for rice cultivation. Soon rice became a staple grain and it was eaten daily, cooked with meat and curd or boiled with pulses to make *khichdi*. The taste for this simple dish of rice and pulses doesn't seem to have diminished over the centuries and it is still a common dish in Delhi and around India. You might like to make a pot of khichdi and imagine that a similar dish was enjoyed in Indraprastha. (Alas we cannot know exactly what the ancient Aryan version may have tasted like as there are no recipes recorded from that period.)

■ *Khichdi* ■
Serves 2-4

Ingredients
1-2 cups rice
1-2 cups husked moong beans (moong dal) or other dal
1-2 tsp turmeric powder
1 tsp ground roasted cumin seeds
2 tsp grated or finely chopped fresh ginger (do not
substitute with ginger powder)
1-2 tsp salt
6 cups water

Method
Pick over and wash rice and dal.

Combine all ingredients together in a pan and cook over low heat until rice and dal are cooked and the khichdi has the consistency of thick porridge.

You can serve the khichdi with some melted ghee or butter to enrich it.

The Aryans also enjoyed rice parched and flattened or puffed up into crispy orbs.

You can still find these rice products in Delhi in several forms—as part of a *namkeen* or *chaat* such as bhel puri, or used in dishes such as *poha*.

■ *Poha* ■
Serves 6

Ingredients
2 cups chidwa (flattened rice)
1 tbsp vegetable oil

1 tbsp mustard seeds
8 curry leaves
1 small onion, diced
$^1/_2$ cup cooked and diced carrot
$^1/_2$ cup cooked peas
4 small potatoes, boiled, skinned and cut into small cubes
salt to taste
2 tbsp lemon juice
$^1/_2$ cup roasted chickpeas for garnish
1 tsp turmeric

Method

Soak chidwa in enough water to cover it for 30 seconds. Drain well.

Heat oil over high heat. Add mustard seeds and cook until they pop. Add mustard seeds and cook until they pop. Add curry leaves and spices and cook for 1 minute. Lower heat, add onion and cook until slightly softened. Add carrots and peas and cook for 1 minute. Add potato and stir through. Add drained chidwa, stir well and cook for 1 minute.

Add salt and lemon juice to taste and garnish with chickpeas.

Although some of the descriptions of the architecture of ancient Delhi in the *Mahabharata* are clearly fantastical, the descriptions of food seem to be more on a par with reality. Early on in the work we find the inhabitants of Indraprastha enjoying simple feasts of *roasted meat dressed generously with curd*. As the story continues and Indraprastha develops, the food becomes more elaborate. Roastd meats remain the mainstay of the diet but these are now enhanced with *sauces of tamarind, pomegranate, ghee, salt, herbs, spices, black pepper* and *mangoes*. Additional flavours were added with garnishes of *radish, citrus fruit, asafoetida* (hing) and *ginger.*

Rice snacks at a Bengali store, Chittaranjan Park

As with all significant cuisines, Aryan cooking gathered complexity and incorporated new ingredients over time and the food depicted in this *Mahabharata* feast is the product of centuries of development. This feast is also a reflection of the food of the kayasths who set the *Mahabharata* in writing between 500 BC and 500 AD.[6] The kayasths were very fond of eating meat, as were all the Hindu castes, but around 500 BC there began to be a change in the Hindu attitude towards meat consumption. The

---

[6]The *Mahabharata* spent nearly 1000 years as an oral treatise before it was put down in writing.

later chapters of the *Mahabharata* state that only food grains are suitable for ritual sacrifice whereas earlier chapters prescribed a long list of animals that were deemed suitable for sacrifice and consumption. This change reflected not only the growing influence of Buddhism and Jainism in India in the centuries just prior to the birth of Christ but also that an agrarian society heavily dependent on their cattle found animal slaughter expensive and uneconomical.

By 500 BC the Hindu caste system was fully 'operational'. Many people found themselves disadvantaged by the arbitrary nature of this system and resented the extraordinary powers that the caste system vested in the Brahmin or priestly caste. Both Buddhism and Jainism grew out of Hinduism but both were 'caste free' and these religions began to attract popular followings. The Buddha delivered two important sermons near Delhi around 500 BC and he is recorded to have said that the food people consumed in Indraprastha was influenced by Buddhist principles. As the Buddha preached a philosophy of 'non-violence' (which meant not killing animals for food or sacrifice but that meat could be eaten if the animal had been accidentally killed), it could be assumed that the slaughtering of animals for consumption must have been significantly reduced in Indraprastha during this time.

But it was not only those citizens of Indraprastha who were influenced by the Buddha or Mahavira who had stopped eating meat. In an attempt to deflect the potential impact of these competing religions, Hinduism simply began to absorb some of the more popular elements of these. For the high-caste Brahmins, who had traditionally conducted the ritual animal sacrifices that had been required to propitiate the Hindu gods, it became meritorious to be vegetarian. This led to a general feeling of revulsion towards eating meat in Hindu society. Meat-eating did not stop altogether. Other castes continued to eat meat and the very lowest castes even ate the meat of certain reptiles. However, vegetarianism gradually became prevalent in Hindu culture. Pious Hindus also stopped eating onions, garlic and leek as the pungent nature of these vegetables was considered to create negative energy within the body leaving the body and breath with a bad odour. Instead they began to use the strong-smelling resin, asafoetida which had come into India from Afghanistan, as a substitute.

By the beginning of the first millennium AD, the basis of Indian food was laid down: *boiled rice served with well-spiced sauces* (the 'curry' of modern cookery terms); cooked and ground *pulses* (dal); *rice cooked with milk; flesh* (for those who ate it) *cooked with curd and spices.* Dairy products were of prime importance in both vegetarian and non-vegetarian cooking; and were liberally added to both sweet and savoury dishes in the form of *ghee, curd* and *milk* (which came from buffaloes, goats and sheep). *Sugar, honey* and *jaggery* were all used as sweeteners and the preparation of sweets was well developed. Sweet dishes that combined dairy products and sugar such as shrikand were well loved by the Aryans and this ancient dish is enjoyed even today.

■ *Shrikand* ■
Serves 6

Ingredients
$^1/_2$ tsp saffron strings
1 tbsp warm milk
$^3/_4$ cup sugar or jaggery powder or 3-4 tbsp honey
3 cups hung curd*
2 tbsp crushed pistachio nuts
$^1/_2$ tsp ground green cardamom seeds

Method
Dissolve saffron in milk.
Add sweetener to curd and beat well with a whisk.
Blend in remaining ingredients.
Chill before serving.
*To make hung curd, place curd in a muslin cloth and hang cloth for 5-6 hours for the liquid to drain out.

Another common sweet was sesame mixed with treacle or honey and pressed into cakes. Modern variations on this ancient confection, called *gujak,* are still sold by street vendors all over Delhi (a common variation is made with peanuts which was a much later entry to India). Gujak is very simple to make.

■ *Gujak* ■
Makes 500 g

Ingredients
1 tbsp ghee or vegetable oil
2 cups jaggery/gur
2 cups roasted peanuts (skin removed) or toasted
sesame seeds

Method
Heat ghee or oil in a pan and add jaggery. Cook till the hardball
stage (a small amount of the hot syrup forms a firm ball when
dropped into some iced water).

Add peanuts or sesame seeds, stir briskly and pour onto
a greased surface or tray. It will harden as it cools.

Cut into squares or diamonds or break into pieces. Store
in an airtight container.

In nearly every restaurant in Delhi, great and small, one
can enjoy a simple meal of *dal, rice, roti* and *sabzi*. This
meal has its roots in ancient India and is the staple Indian
diet. If you would like to sample more orthodox Hindu
dishes that are pure vegetarian and made without onion
and garlic or mushrooms (considered to be impure as they
grow on compost) then you could visit **Govindas**. Located
in the huge Iskcon Temple that dominates the skyline in
Sant Nagar, the food here is not only pure vegetarian but
is also karma free (as it is offered to the gods as *prasad*
before being served). Hindus believe that food not only
nourishes the body but the soul as well, and that spiritual

purity can be heightened or tainted by the foods one consumes. The atmosphere in this busy restaurant is not a pious one though, and the array of dishes offered (the menu changes daily) is an education for those who cannot imagine cooking without onion or garlic. (Don't be surprised if a sense of well-being envelops you after a meal here!)

Delhi Ka Aangan is more concerned with man's material well-being than his spiritual one but you will still find a range of skilfully prepared pure vegetarian (no onion or garlic) dishes on the menu such as *palak ki nazabal* (spinach patties with paneer, cashews, dried fruit and poppy seeds), *dal arhar kaeri* (yellow lentils with green mango tempered with cumin seeds), *jeera aloo* (a simple dish of potato cooked with cumin seeds that tastes far more elaborate than it is) and *aloo khaas tikki* (potato patties filled with spiced lentils with a yogurt, mint and tamarind chutney); ancient flavours turned into modern ambrosia.

To the modern gourmet, the Hindu food ethos may seem somewhat restrictive (although tasting should reveal otherwise) but the Jain food ethos is even more austere. Jains revere all life including that of insects and microscopic organisms. Not only do they not consume any flesh, onion, garlic, leeks or mushrooms, they also do not eat any root vegetables; any pickle more than three days old; honey; any food that is red such as tomato, radish and carrot (as red is the colour of blood), or eggplant or cabbage and vegetables that are likely to have worms or other life forms clinging to their leaves. During the monsoon months when the 'life forces' are said to be at their peak (translated this means that there is abundant insect life at this time and these could be accidentally killed), orthodox Jains will not eat any green leafy vegetables and may choose not to eat any vegetables at all (with the exception of vegetables that have been previously dried). Jains prefer dry food like grains and cereals as 'wet' food (fruit), may harbour life forms or even mould. *Paan* is not taken by Jains as the lime paste that the leaf is spread with may be made from ground shells and the decorative silver leaf (*varak*) that is found on many Indian sweets is not eaten as it is beaten out between soft leather or cow intestines. This begs the question, 'What do Jains eat?' The answer to that lies in busy Karol Bagh (unless you are well acquainted with a Jain cook), at **Suruchi** restaurant. Here you can enjoy a *thali* made up of Jain dishes such as *bhindi masala* (spicy lady's finger), *kathor matar* (white peas cooked with coconut and asafoetida) and *methi gheza* (methi leaves cooked with *besan*, *zeera*, green chillies, salt and curd). The food at Suruchi is exceptionally delicious and servings are endless; in fact the staff seem determined that no one should leave without a thoroughly sustaining feed. The *kudi* that accompanies these dishes is a typical Jain dish; it is also very moorish.

■ *Kudi* ■
Serves 4-6

Ingredients
1 cup plain curd
1¹/₂ cups water
1 tbsp gram flour (besan)
salt to taste
1 tsp ghee
1-2 tsp cumin seeds
3 cloves
1 green chilli
a pinch of asafoetida (hing)
1-2 tbsp jaggery/gur

Method
Blend curd, water, gram flour and salt.

Heat ghee in a pan, and add cumin and cloves. Fry for a few moments. Add chilli and cook until it darkens. Add asafoetida, then curd mixture. Bring to boil stirring continuously. Turn heat down to simmer and cook gently for 10-15 minutes stirring occasionally. Add jaggery.

Serve in a *katori* as part of a thali or as an accompaniment with rice.

You might also find some of these delectable croquettes on your thali—Jains commonly substitute mashed plantain (a starchy mild-tasting variety of banana) for potato.

■ *Jain Croquettes* ■
Serves 6

Ingredients
4 tbsp semolina
3 plantains

1 cup paneer, finely crumbled
4 green chillies, finely chopped
1 tsp chaat masala (see chapter 'Street food, Snacks and
Sweets' for recipe)
salt to taste
vegetable oil for deep frying

Method

Cook plantains in their skin until soft. Peel and mash.

Add paneer, chillies and chaat masala and mix thoroughly.
Allow to cool slightly.

Dry-roast semolina until golden. Keep aside 2 tbsp.

Add 2 tbsp water to remaining semolina and stir until
smooth. Mix into plantain mixture with salt to taste.

Shape into croquettes. Dust with reserved semolina. Chill
for an hour.

Deep fry in hot oil until golden.

No form of the name Delhi (Dhilli, Dilli, Dhilluka etc)
can be traced before the year AD 7 and any history of the
city before that time remains murky. The first settlements
to be known by the name Delhi (or a variation of) were
established in the area near where the Qutab Minar stands
today. By AD 676, Ang Pal I, a Tomar Rajput, was
established as the ruler of Delhi. The Rajputs were the
traditional ruling and warrior class of northern India and
until 1192, various Rajput clans ruled over Delhi. The
Rajputs were Hindus but as befits their warrior status, were
very fond of *shikar* (hunting) and meat was an important
component of their diet. The lands around Delhi were
rich with game and wildlife in the first millennium AD and

the ruling Rajputs would have had plenty of opportunity to indulge in their passion for this sport (centuries later they were to lead the Mughal Emperor Akbar on hunting expeditions in the Delhi area). Unlike the later Mughals, the Rajputs did not set out on their game expeditions with an enormous entourage of cooks, bearers and kitchen tents. Instead they choose to enjoy their catch in situ, typically roasted over an open fire or turned into simple dishes that employed a minimum of ingredients and fuss: *lal maas* is a popular Rajput dish that evolved out of this combination. The 'lal' of this dish is a hearty dose of red chilli. Delhi's ruling Rajputs did not have chillies but as this dish evolved over time they have become an integral part of its appeal. You can try this dish at home, although a trip to the butcher to procure some meat will have to substitute for the hunting.

■ *Lal Maas* ■
Serves 4

Ingredients
1 cup vegetable oil
2 tsp chopped garlic
$1^1/_2$ tsp cumin seeds
seeds of 5 green cardamom, crushed
seeds of 5 black cardamom, crushed
4-6 whole red chillies or to taste
1 onion, finely sliced
500 g mutton or lamb, cut into 5-cm pieces
2 tsp red chilli powder

2 tsp coriander powder
2 tsp salt
1 cup curd beaten smooth with a fork

Method

Heat oil in a pan. Add garlic, cumin seeds, cardamoms and whole red chillies. Fry until cumin seeds begin to sputter. Add onions and cook until golden brown.

Add meat and cook over high heat until meat is sealed. Mix in remaining ingredients and a cup of water.

Cover pan and cook over low heat for 45 minutes or until meat is tender and the flavour well developed.

If you crave a taste of the hunt but would rather that someone else did the cooking, then **Urban Nomads** serves an authentic version of *lal maas*. This relaxed eatery has an earthy interior of muted green walls and a stone floor that assist in creating a rustic ambience in which one can enjoy this unpretentious dish. (The discreetly displayed designer clothing and glamorous accessories give comfort to those who don't want to move too far from their urban environment.)

The Rajputs are just as renowned for their inter-clan rivalry as they are for their love of hunting. Delhi's early Rajput rulers were no exception. Constantly embroiled in internal feuding they were ill-prepared for external attack, and when the mountain passes of the Hindukush disgorged the war-loving Turks of Central Asia onto India's fertile plains, they swiftly captured Delhi from her Hindu potentates. By 1192, the Rajputs had retreated back to their desert strongholds and Muslim rule began in Delhi.

GOVINDAS
Iskcon, Sant Nagar Main
Road, East of Kailash,
Near C-Block Market
26280069
Noon-3 p.m. & 7 a.m.-10 p.m.

DELHI KA AANGAN
Hyatt Recency
Bikaji Cama Place
Ring Road
26181234
12.30-3.00 p.m. &
7.30 a.m.-11 p.m.

URBAN NOMADS
Chiranjiv Tower
43 Nehru Place
26420982, 26420983
11 a.m.-11 p.m.

SURUCHI RESTAURANT
15A/56 W.E.A Karol Bagh
(Hotel Swagat)
25731615, 25731617
8 a.m.-11 p.m.

■ Suggested tour ($^1/_2$ day)

There is little direct evidence of Ancient Delhi in the city itself so the best place to start is the National Museum on Janpath. The museum houses a significant collection of artefacts from the Harappan era, which includes a number of cooking utensils and pots. It is worth seeing these if only to witness how little Indian cooking implements have changed since 2000 BC.

When you have finished at the museum, head down Rajpath to the Purana Qila (Old Fort). The fort is a piece of Mughal architecture and was part of Humayun's city of Din-i-Panah (completed in 1538). The fort was the citadel of a city, which in its heyday spread down to the Yamuna and north to Firoz Shah Kotla. It is this site though, rather than the fort, that is of importance in the context of Ancient Delhi, for it is on this spot that Indraprastha is considered to have stood.

There has been significant archaeological work done on the Purana Qila site and there is evidence of ancient habitation here. A small archaeological museum in the Purana Qila houses some of the artefacts that have been dug up here. When the British began building their city of New Delhi in the early decades of the twentieth century, they cleared away a small village adjacent to this site that was known locally as Indraprastha. You will have to let your imagination picture the ancient settlement that may have existed here.

For a culinary accompaniment to your exploration of early Delhi you will need to look out for street vendors selling as *aloo* and *split pea tikkis* and *gujak* (sesame and peanut versions).

The most significant remains of Delhi's Rajput era are at Surajkund. This site is 17 km outside of the city proper and there are the remains of a temple, an amphitheatre and a large stepwell, all considered to have been built by the Rajputs. An internationally renowned **crafts mela** is held here every February at which you can also sample a variety of traditional food from across India—definitely worth a visit.

National Museum

Open 10 a.m. to 5 p.m. daily; closed on Mondays.
Entrance fee is Rs 10 for Indians, Rs 150 for foreigners.

Surajkund

This is a half-day excursion in itself, all day if you are visitng the crafts mela. During the mela there are buses from central Delhi to Surajkund but at other times you will need to go there in a private car or taxi. You head south on the Mehrauli-Badarpur Road which goes past Tughlaqabad Fort.

Two

■

SULTANATE DELHI

■ The Delhi Sultans

1206 Qutab-ud-din Aibak
1229 Iltutmish
1266–1287 Balban
1296–1316 Alauddin Khilji
1316–1320 Khusrau Khan
1320–1324 Ghiyas-ud-din Tughlaq
1324–51 Muhammad bin Tughlaq
1351–1388 Firoz Shah Tughlaq
1395–1414 Mahmud Tughlaq
1414–1451 Sayyid Dynasty
1451–1526 Lodi Dynasty

In 1220 the Muslim call to prayer rang out from the towering heights of the newly completed Qutab Minar; Delhi was now an Islamic city. The Turks who had captured Delhi were not the first Muslims to venture into India. There had been Arab merchants and traders living in Gujarat and along the Malabar Coast for several centuries, but the Turks were the first Muslims to found a city in

India. Of the same Central Asian stock as the Ottomans who founded Turkey, the Turks had come to India from the isolated mountain regions of Afghanistan. The Turks were only relatively recent converts to Islam when they took Delhi. Zealous in their new-found faith and eager to demonstrate their orthodoxy, they set about refashioning Delhi into an Islamic city. They tore down the temples of the Hindu 'infidels' and used the materials to build their own places of worship. Perhaps mindful of local legend, they installed the iron pillar of Delhi in the courtyard of the Quwwat-ul-Islam mosque.[1]

The Turks gave their rulers the title 'Sultan' (Muslim sovereign) and thus began the rule of the Delhi Sultanate. Several of Delhi's early Sultans had been slaves and the early Sultanate era is also referred to as the 'Slave Dynasty'.

The Turks who became Delhi's reigning Sultans were not, by heritage, a refined fraternity. Their nomadic ancestors in the Central Asian steppes had bequeathed them with well-developed survival skills but few cultural nuances. As wandering warriors, the Turks had prided themselves on their martial skills and practicality but the height of their culinary sophistication would have been a *roasted sheep* and a draught of *fermented ewe's milk*. As the Sultans began to develop Delhi they realized that to

---

[1] The pillar commemorates the heroic deeds of a fifth-century Hindu ruler and is considered a symbol for the stability of Delhi.

make it a truly great Islamic city it needed a cultural plan as well as a material one. Lacking a refined cultural model of their own the Sultans had to look elsewhere for inspiration; and what better place to look but the urbane courts of medieval Persia.

The culture of Persia was a reference point for Muslims of the middle ages, and the Persians were often called the Frenchmen of the East. The culinary arts enjoyed an elevated place in Persian courtly life, ranking as high as poetry in cultural importance and food was a subject on which Persian poetry often dwelt. Persian nobles were expected to be knowledgeable about culinary matters and hosting elaborate feasts was a social requirement for an aspiring courtier.

The food of the Persian courts was rich and elaborate: nuts were used to enrich dishes and thicken sauces; mutton fat was the favourite cooking medium; both savoury and sweet dishes were perfumed with the distilled essences of rose petals, orange blossom and *kewra* (screwpine); spices were added to create subtlety and depth and citrus, dried fruit and mint were liberally used for both flavour and garnish. However, the Sultans did not lose their taste for the meat and milk diet of their past in their quest for refinement.

The Delhi Sultans had little trouble replicating Persian culinary mores. They recruited Persian cooks to come to Delhi and many of the basic foods of Persian cuisine were already available in India. The spices that the Persians were so fond of came to them from India via the Arab spice trade. Other important Persian foods such as sesame, wheat and honey had been eaten in India for more than a millennia prior to the arrival of the Sultans. The arable land surrounding Delhi was in marked contrast to the deserts and rugged mountains of Persia; most produce that grew in that climate could be easily and abundantly grown around Delhi. What could not be grown was imported— money was no object in fulfilling the desires of the Delhi court. The Persian-inspired dishes of *meat cooked with rice*, *nuts* and *fruit* that have become synonymous with Delhi cuisine were first served in the courts of the Sultans. The flavours of Sultanate Delhi are captured in this *biryani* recipe.

■ *Biryani* ■
Serves 10-12

Ingredients
5 cups (750 g) basmati rice or long-grain white rice
a generous pinch of saffron threads
1 cup ghee
2 onions, finely sliced
50 g unsalted raw cashew nuts
50 g unsalted pistachio nuts
50 g sultanas or seedless raisins
50 g dried apricots, finely diced
10-cm piece ginger, finely grated
4-6 cloves garlic, crushed

1 tsp cumin seeds
1 kg mutton or lamb cut into 5-cm pieces
salt
3-cm stick cinnamon, broken into 2-3 pieces
6 cloves
6 black peppercorns
seeds of 4 green cardamoms, crushed
a pinch of mace flakes or $^1/_2$ tsp ground mace
1 cup curd
$1^1/_2$ litres chicken/mutton/lamb stock or water
rose water or kewra essence (optional)

Method

Cook rice in plenty of boiling salted water for 10 minutes. Drain and set aside.

Soak saffron in 2 tsp boiling hot water for 10 minutes.

Heat three-quarters of the ghee in a heavy based casserole dish over the stove top on medium heat. Fry onions until crisp and golden, then remove from ghee with a slotted spoon and drain on kitchen paper.

Add nuts and dried fruit to ghee and cook until nuts are lightly browned. Remove with a slotted spoon and drain on kitchen paper.

Add ginger, garlic and cumin to ghee (adding the remaining ghee if needed) and cook until cumin seeds start to sputter. Add meat and salt and cook until meat pieces are brown. Add cinnamon, cloves, peppercorns, cardamom, mace, curd and about $2^1/_2$ cups stock. Stir through meat mixture thoroughly. Cook over moderate heat for 45 minutes or until meat is tender.

Remove meat from casserole dish with a slotted spoon and pour the cooking liquid into another dish.

Place a layer of rice in casserole dish, then a layer of meat. Spread another layer of rice and the remainder of the meat.

Cover with remaining rice. Gently pour reserved cooking liquid and remaining stock over the rice. Sprinkle saffron and its liquid on top.

Cover casserole with a sheet of foil and put on the lid, crimping the edges of the foil around the lid. Or make a thick flour and water paste and seal the edges of the casserole with this paste (the Delhi Sultans were not familiar with aluminium foil!).

Bake in an oven preheated to 160°C for 35-45 minutes or until all the liquid has been absorbed by the rice.

Stir biryani to mix everything through. Sprinkle with reserved onions, nuts and dried fruit.

If you like you can add a sprinkle of *kewra* or rose water over the biryani before serving.

To further fulfil their cultural aspirations, the Delhi Sultans added Persian nobles to the inner circles of their court. It was going to take more than Persian aristocracy though to establish Muslim dominance in Delhi—and by design India—and the early Sultans actively encouraged the immigration of educated Muslims. Generous endowments for the provision of Muslim travellers were made and any accomplished or professional Muslim who made the journey to Delhi was handsomely rewarded.

In 1334, during the reign of Sultan Muhammad bin Tughlaq, the 'traveller of the age', Ibn Battuta, arrived in Delhi. A native of Tangier, Battuta was on a personal pilgrimage to visit all the regions of the world where Muslims ruled or had settled. Word of the splendour of Delhi and the generous reception he could expect there must have made the city particularly appealing to him. It is fortunate for us that Ibn Battuta visited Delhi, for it is his lively and engaging tales that give us the foremost picture of culinary life in Sultanate Delhi. Unlike the odes commissioned by the Sultans—where the focus is on their great deeds and glorious battles—Battuta's chronicles document the minutiae of daily life.

Battuta was by profession a qadi (an Islamic law giver or judge) and it was incumbent on any Muslim ruler to offer him hospitality. Eager to fulfil his duties as a devout Muslim and to demonstrate the potential of his patronage, Muhammad bin Tughlaq welcomed Battuta with 5,000 dinars and a house in Palam. The Sultan's mother hosted a lavish feast in honour of Battuta (she did not actually attend the feast confined as she was in purdah), and the Sultan employed Battuta as a *qadi* even though Battuta spoke only Arabic and the language of the Delhi court was Persian.

To assist him in settling down, the Sultan sent Battuta a 'hospitality gift': *1000 pounds of Indian flour, one third of it mira, that is fine flour, and two thirds in khushlar, that is coarsely ground flour; a thousand pounds of flesh-meat and I cannot say how many pounds of sugar, ghee, salit* [probably saleb, a powder made from a type of orchid used in a popular drink in the Middle East but not common in Delhi any more] *and areca nuts, with a thousand betel leaves.* The contents of this gift were to enable him to feed his

household, for although Battuta always refers to himself
in the singular, he would have arrived in Delhi with an
entourage of people: slave girls, servants, grooms and
bearers. The food would have also allowed him to offer
hospitality to others.

Battuta's elevated position as a *qadi* meant that he
was able to enjoy the ostentatious lifestyle of a Delhi
noble. It was a way of living that emulated that of the
Sultan: palatial homes, gold and silver tableware, exquisite
tapestries and carpets and extravagance with food. The
necessity of maintaining such a lifestyle meant that Battuta
was always in debt but so were all the other Delhi nobles;
it was par for the course. The cardinal point of Delhi life
in the Sultanate period was the Sultan's court and Battuta's
position amongst Delhi's elite also allowed him to become
an acquisitive observer of its proceedings.

When the Sultan was in residence in Delhi—he was
often away hunting or fighting battles—he hosted feasts
twice a day; there was both a public and a private feast.
The public meals were held in the Sultan's hall of audience
and all of Delhi's worthy citizens and any distinguished
visitors were expected to attend these public feasts (men
only). Guests were required to be punctual and present
during the arrival of the food. When the food was carried
in to the hall it was accompanied with much formality.
Chamberlains cried out *Bismillah* (In the name of Allah)
and everybody present had to rise. An oration of effusive

praise for the Sultan's generosity was made by a senior *naqib* (official), followed by an elaborate homage to the Sultan; then a second oration of praise followed the first. A written report of the arrival of the food was presented to the Sultan even though, as Battuta notes, 'he already [knew] of its arrival'. On receipt of the written report, the Sultan appointed an *amir* (a noble) to assign places to the guests and preside over the distribution of the food. It was important that each man be seated according to his rank as it was this that determined the quantity of food he received and the quality of his tableware.

The meal began with *rose-water-flavoured sharbat* served in 'gold, silver, brass and glass' vessels (according to rank). Once this was drunk, the eating could begin. Each person present would be assigned an individual platter and a portion of each dish served would be placed on the platter. There was no sharing of food between guests. *Roast meat*, two types of *bread*: 'thin rounds of bread' (chapati) and 'cakes of bread soaked in ghee', *rice cooked with chicken* and *samusak* (samosa) were served. A sweet dish and *fuqqa* (a mildly alcoholic drink brewed from barley) rounded off the meal.

Samosas were most likely a Hindu food item that found its way into the Sultan's court after his Muslim cooks had enriched them with meat and nuts. The crisp ghee-rich pastry filled with spiced meat made them a great favourite with the Delhi aristocracy—no doubt they were also prized in the fourteenth century for their exotic and novel value. Over the subsequent centuries, samosas have found their way from the Sultanate court onto the streets of Delhi where numerous samosawallahs sell them freshly fried, hot and delicious. In Old Delhi you will get samosas filled with *keema*; elsewhere in the city they will be most commonly filled with potato. Or you can try your hand at making them yourself as part of a Sultanate-inspired feast.

■ *Sharbat-e-Gulab (Rose Cordial)* ■
Makes about 500 ml

Rose cordial is easily available in gorcery stores. You can mix it with cold water, soda or milk. But if you happen to have an excess of fresh, scented rose petals, you can make your own. To each 500 g of rose petals you will need 2 kg sugar.

Wash the petals well (ensure that you have only petals and have removed any stems or leaves). Put the petals in a saucepan and cover with water. Cook over a medium heat until the water has reduced by half. Strain the liquid and discard the petals. Add the sugar to the liquid and bring to boil. Reduce heat and cook until the liquid has the consistency of a syrup. Cool and bottle.

You can add 1 tbsp of rose water to enhance the rose flavour (add when the syrup has cooled). You may also add a drop or two of pink food colouring if you like.

■ *Samosa* ■
Makes 35-40 pieces
Pastry:

Ingredients
2 cups plain flour (maida)
1 tsp salt
3 tbsp melted ghee or vegetable oil (ghee is best)
5-6 tsp very cold water or buttermilk

Method
Sift flour and salt together. Add ghee or oil and enough water
or buttermilk to make a soft dough. Knead until smooth.
Cover with a damp tea towel and set aside for 30 minutes.

Filling:

Ingredients
$1/2$ tsp saffron strings
2 tbsp honey
3 tbsp ghee
5-cm piece ginger, finely grated
1 onion, very finely diced
4-6 cloves garlic, crushed
salt and pepper to taste
450 g minced mutton or lamb
$1/2$ tsp ground nutmeg
$1/2$ cup finely chopped almonds, walnuts and pistachio
nuts

Method
Crush saffron strings into honey.
 Heat ghee in a frying pan over medium heat and add ginger,
onion, garlic and salt. Fry until onion is soft and golden. Add
meat and saffron-infused honey. Stir until meat is cooked
through. Add nutmeg, reduce heat and cook uncovered until
any liquid is gone and filling is firm and dryish but not
completely dried out. Stir in nuts.

To assemble

Pinch off a small walnut-size piece of dough. Roll into a ball and then roll out into a flat circle with a rolling pin. Cut circle in half. (Sometimes I cheat and just roll out all the dough thinly and cut the circles out with a cutter!)

Moisten cut edge with water and shape into a cone. Fill with a 2-3 tsp of filling. Press down top edge and crimp edge with a fork.

Deep fry in ghee until golden. Serve hot.

■ Sheermal ■

Makes 5-6

This rich bread is a Muslim favourite. While it lacks a 'honey, almond and sesame topping', it is a sweet bread that is served with a liberal soaking of ghee on the top.

Ingredients

500 g plain flour (maida)
1 tsp salt
2 tsp baking powder
3 tbsp sugar
1 cup warm milk
$^1/_2$ cup ghee

Method

Sieve flour with salt and baking powder, and mix in sugar.

Sprinkle milk over flour and knead to a soft dough. Cover with a damp cloth and set aside for 30 minutes in a warm place.

Melt ghee and knead into dough on a well-floured surface until it is smooth and elastic.

Shape dough into 5 or 6 balls. Flatten balls into $1^1/_2$-cm thick rounds and prick all over with a fork.

Sheermal are traditionally baked in a tandoor oven. You

can bake them in a moderate Western-style oven but for better results cook them in a heavy-based frying pan until golden brown on both sides. Sprinkle with a little extra milk just before they are completely cooked (this gives them a nice golden coat).

When still hot brush liberally with extra melted ghee. You could give them a lick of honey as well if it takes your fancy.

Although the Sultan was considered to reign over these public meals, he generally did not attend them. While the public meal was in progress, the Sultan ate his meal in his private sitting room in the company of a small group of select people. It was a mark of great distinction and favour to be a part of the Sultan's private meals—a privilege that Battuta enjoyed on many occasions during his Delhi residency. If the Sultan wished to confer further honour on one of his guests during the meal he would take a plate, place a piece of bread on it and give it to the person he wished to acknowledge.[1] The recipient would then pick up the bread in his left hand and pay homage to the Sultan with his right hand to the ground. If the Sultan wished to honour a person not present at the private dinner he would send a portion of the food to that person. On receipt of such food, this person would also pay homage to the Sultan

---

[1] It was very rare, when giving or receiving, that a Muslim ruler actually touched anything with his own hand. This tradition was a great source of frustration for the British when the Muslim Mughal Emperors would not accept their petitions directly.

in the presence of his company (if he didn't carry out the required rituals he could be certain that one of his dining companions would report such insolence to the right authority).

Both the Sultan's public and private meals always finished with *betel* and *areca nuts*. Each person was given a spoonful of powdered betel nut and 'fifteen leaves of betel tied in a bunch with red silk thread'. The habit of chewing betel leaf and areca nut together—paan as it is more commonly known—is an ancient one. *Areca catechu* is the nut of a variety of palm tree and the betel leaf comes from the climbing vine, *piper betel.* Both species, as well as the habit of chewing paan came to India via early trade with South East Asia. Chewing paan was a Hindu habit unknown to the Muslims before they came to Delhi but it was a habit that they promptly appropriated as part of their culture.

To prepare a paan, the betel leaf is slaked with a little lime paste, some chopped betel nut and spices are added and the leaf is wrapped into a triangular parcel (other ingredients that may be added include coconut, dates, melon seeds). Older betel leaves are preferred to young ones. An alkaloid in the betel nut is released by the lime paste and this is responsible for the characteristic red juice that develops upon chewing it. Habitual paan chewers have teeth dyed red from this juice and are often in the habit of spitting out streams of lurid red saliva. Those eager to demonstrate their spending ability—Sultans, emperors, modern-day movie stars and politicians—often have expensive aphrodisiacs such as crushed pearl added to their paan. Chewing tobacco (zarda) is commonly added to paan. (This is not a pleasant experience if you are unused to it as it makes your head spin and stings your mouth.) If you choose to have chewing tobacco in your paan, you should spit out the juice as it is quite noxious. The addition of tobacco is not one the Delhi Sultans would have experienced though, as tobacco did not come to India until the sixteenth century.

Chewing paan stimulates saliva, aids digestion and cleanses the mouth and breath after a meal. Given the Muslim love of food rich in ghee and onion, it is no wonder that they took so readily to paan-chewing. For the uninitiated it may seem an incongruous habit to chew a leaf full of spices but it is a most refreshing experience after a meal. The betel nut also has gentle intoxicating properties and is reputed to be addictive. The odd paan however, does no harm and doesn't lead to a mouth full of red teeth—it takes some dedication to the habit to achieve that.

In the Sultanate era, giving paan to another became an auspicious sign of hospitality. Muhammad bin Tughlaq set up pavilions where any citizen could help himself to sharbat (set out in 'tanks' made from animal skins), betel leaves and areca nuts. The popularity of chewing paan has not diminished with the centuries and you can easily find a paanwallah on the streets of modern Delhi. Dedicated paan aficionados will have their favourite vendor, but novices might like to try **Prince Paan** in GK I M-Block market or **Panchayat** in Connaught Place. Both these places are very clean and very popular. Panchayat has the added distinction of being one of the few places in India where women make paan and it is the only place in Delhi where you can buy paan in an air-conditioned shop. The ladies at Panchayat will make up various paans for anything that may ail you—from a sore throat to impotence. The paanwallah outside Sweets Corner in **Sunder Nagar** is also reputable.

Despite Battuta's privileged place amongst Delhi's inner circle, it was necessary to continually court the Sultan's favour to maintain such a position (Muhammad bin Tughlaq was particularly erratic; some days he was 'mad, bad and dangerous to know', on others he was fair, equitable and compassionate). Noting the Sultan's love of sweet things, Battuta arranged for an array of elaborate sweetmeats prepared by his own cook to be sent to him. The Sultan then summoned Battuta for an audience:

He then asked me about a particular kind of the sweetmeats which I had sent him previously. I said to him, 'O Master of the World, those sweetmeats were of many kinds and I do not know which kind you are asking about.' He said, 'Bring those plates' (for they call a platter a plate) and when they brought them and laid them before him and removed their covers, he said, 'It was about this one that I asked' and took the dish in which it was. I said to him, 'This kind is called al-muqarrasa,' then he took another kind and said, 'What is the name of this?' and then I said to him 'These are the judges sweet mouthfuls.' Now there was present a merchant, one of the sheikhs of Baghdad, called al-Samarri . . . . This man was jealous of me, and wishing to humiliate me said, 'These are not the judges sweet mouthfuls, but those are,' and he took a piece of the kind which is called jild-al-faras. There was opposite him the 'king' of the intimate courtiers . . . and he said to him, 'O khoja, you lie and it is the qadi who speaks the truth.' The Sultan said to him, 'How so?' He replied, 'O Master of the World, he is the qadi [judge] and these are his sweet mouthfuls, for he brought them' and the Sultan laughed and said, 'You are right.'[2]

■   *The Judges Sweet Mouthfuls*   ■
Makes 15 pieces

Sugar Syrup

Ingredients
1 kg sugar
1 litre water
few drops rose water (optional)

Method
Combine sugar and water in a pan over moderate heat and

---

[2]Gibb, H.A.R., trans., *The Travels of Ibn Battuta*, vol. III (London: Cambridge University Press, 1971).

stir till sugar dissolves. Raise heat to high and bring to boil rapidly for 15 minutes. Remove sum, cool and add rose water.

Sweet Mouthfuls:

Ingredients
$1^1/_2$ tsp ($7^1/_2$ g) dried yeast or 3 tsp (15g) fresh yeast
$2^1/_2$ cups lukewarm water
1 tsp sugar
$3^1/_2$ cups plain flour
oil for deep frying

Method
Dissolve yeast in $^1/_4$ cup lukewarm water. Add sugar, cover bowl and set aside in a warm spot until the yeast rises and foams.

Sift flour into a bowl.

Beat remaining water into risen yeast mixture. Gradually add flour, beating constantly until the mixture becomes a sticky batter. Cover with plastic wrap and place in a warm spot to rise (approximately $1^1/_4$ hours). Beat mixture vigorously at quarter-hour intervals.

Place at least a 5-cm deep layer of oil in a frying pan and heat. With a wet tsp scoop up the dough or press through a pastry tube and drop into the hot oil.

The balls will swell up and float to the top, lower heat to medium and keep cooking until golden crisp.

Remove balls from oil, drain on absorbent paper and while still hot immerse in sugar syrup.

Muslims are renowned for their love of sweetmeats and syrupy drinks. Even their meat dishes have sweet fruits, or in some instances sugar, added to them. When the Muslims arrived in Delhi they found India's indigenous population familiar with sugar cane and the production of sugar from it. The immediate availability of sugar in Delhi meant that a range of sweetmeats could be easily produced. It is often said that the Muslim love of sweets developed because Islam prohibits the consumption of alcohol and so sweet foods became their 'indulgence'.

The Delhi Sultans may have had the Muslim love of sweets but that didn't curb their taste for alcohol, particularly *wine*. The Sultan's household had a *sharabkhana* (wine cellar), *sharabdar* (cellar master) and *saqi-i-khas* (one who dispenses the liquor). The upkeep of these is testimony to the importance and entrenchment of alcohol consumption in the royal Delhi courts. The wine the Sultans drank was imported from Persia at great cost as grapes were not a common fruit in Delhi during the Sultanate period. Sultan Firoz Shah was noted for his 'deep addiction to wine' and he was very active in developing the cultivation of grapes in the later years of the Delhi Sultanate. Perhaps their status as neo-converts to Islam meant that the Sultans didn't feel the need to heed all Islamic law too closely or perhaps their elevated position made them feel they were exempt from such laws. Replicating their sovereign's habits, the Delhi nobles also held wine-drinking parties in their homes. All this drinking didn't curb their love of sweets though (there goes that theory) and dishes such as *halwa* and *shahi tukra* (see chapter 'Festivals') flourished in the Sultanate period.

Sooji halwa being sold in Nizamuddin

■ *Sooji ka Halwa* ■
Serves 8

Ingredients
$2^1/_2$ cups water
$^3/_4$ cup sugar
5 tbsp ghee (do not substitute as it will not taste as good
if you use anything else)
20-30 almonds, blanched
2 cups semolina
2-3 tbsp sultanas or seedless raisins
seeds of 4 green cardamom, finely crushed

Method
Bring water to boil. Add sugar and keep stirring to dissolve.
Keep the water on a rolling boil.

Heat ghee in a heavy-based pan over medium heat. When
hot, add almonds and fry till lightly brown. Remove with a
slotted spoon and drain on kitchen paper.

Add semolina to ghee and keep stirring until golden.
Slowly start adding sugar syrup. Keep stirring as you add the
syrup. Add sultanas and almonds, keep stirring and cook
over low heat for 5 minutes. Stir in a cardamom.

You can serve this halwa, hot, cold or at room temperature
(but I think it is at its delectable best served hot with a
generous splash of cream).

The distinctively Muslim sweet, *jalebi*, was also introduced
into Delhi during the Sultanate era. These unique sticky
coils of crisp batter are at their calorie-saturated best when
eaten warm, and as jalebiwallahs are typically positioned
at the front of sweet shops, you can enjoy watching

them being freshly made. The saffron-coloured batter is dexterously squeezed out of a pastry bag in a series of spirals into a kadhai of hot oil. The jalebi puffs up, turns golden and is then given a brief bath in a thick sugar syrup. Jalebis are available in sweet shops all over in Delhi but it is in Old Delhi where they are at their authentic best. You will see towering trays of jalebis on the counters of most Chandni Chowk sweet shops. **Old and Famous Jalebiwala** only sells jalebis and, as the name suggests, is the best-known place in Chandni Chowk to enjoy these sweet confections.

The Sultans may have paid little heed to the Koranic law prohibiting alcohol consumption but they did fulfil their religious duty in ensuring that all their subjects had enough to eat. According to Islamic faith, all Muslims are obligated to share their food with others; to ensure that those less fortunate than them are fed and to ensure that no food is wasted. While Delhi's illustrious citizenry were kept well fed by the Sultan's daily feasts, it is unlikely that they ate the entire meal served to them. They would have taken their fill and the remains would have been distributed to others further down the social scale. Much of Delhi's food was grown in the farming districts that surrounded the city. When these areas began to experience periods of severe drought, which then led to food shortages and famine, Muhammad bin Tughlaq froze grain prices and ordered that the 'whole population of Delhi should be given six month supplies from the royal granary'. Battuta also donated much of his abundant daily food allowance to relieve famine victims (thus winning commendation from the Sultan on the strength of which he persuaded the Sultan to 'relieve' him of some of his heavy debts).

Hidden amidst two-storey homes and busy roads of modern Delhi's prosperous southern suburbs is the urban village of **Nizamuddin**. The Sufi saint Shekh Hazrat Nizamuddin lived here in the thirteenth century. He was an important religious figure in his lifetime and this village grew up around him (it was on the outskirts of Sultanate Delhi). His *dargah* (shrine) was built here after his death and it remains one of the most important pilgrimage sites in India. To make your way to the shrine through the compressed and congested alleys of Nizamuddin—people, goats and fat-tailed sheep—is to be transported to a medieval Muslim village. On the far side of the dargah there is a cluster of 'hotels' (restaurant/cafe) serving the type of food that would have been the daily fare of the ordinary Delhi citizen of the Sultanate period: *naan* (bread), *keema* or *kabab*, *rice* with plenty of onions, and sweets such as *phirni* and *kheer* (rice cooked with milk and sugar). Seven centuries later, this simple menu is still the daily fare of much of Delhi's Muslim population. Outside these hotels there are always people grouped on the footpath patiently waiting for a pilgrim to honour his duty as a good Muslim and ensure that they are fed.

Even those of a different faith can ensure that someone is nourished by purchasing a meal ticket from one of the hotel vendors. There is a *langar* (community kitchen/meal) everyday in the dargah which provides a free meal for needy pilgrims who visit the tomb and the poor who spend their days there. During his lifetime, Hazrat Nizamuddin often gave his own food away saying that he couldn't bear to eat while others were starving.

A 'hotel' in Nizamuddin

The arrival of the Muslims in Delhi, and the attendant destruction of the existing monuments and buildings, created major upheaval for Delhi's native Hindu population. Yet, by the time the invaders had established themselves in their recreated city, the Hindus had settled back into their agrarian life outside the ramparts of urban

Delhi. While the Muslims favoured the dense community of the city, the Hindus preferred a rural existence and their ancient role as farmers of the land. The Delhi Sultans were heavily reliant on the Hindus' agricultural prowess for their own wealth and the livelihood of their citizens. All of the land surrounding Delhi was owned and controlled by the Sultan. Any village on that land had to pay tax. The Sultan assigned a village, or a number of villages, to each royal, noble and important person in Delhi and the taxes paid by these villages became their income. These Delhi personages in turn employed a huge number of people to run their households and supplied all their needs from this 'income tax'. The Sultans understood well that agriculture was the backbone of their economy and did not tax the Hindu farmers so heavily as to deprive them of a sufficient livelihood. They also left the Hindu population to live in their self-sufficient villages and they were free to practise their own religion.

Just as the Muslims threw up huge walls around the city to keep the 'infidels' at bay, the Hindus reinforced their own cultural parameters. They resisted any influence from the Muslims in their religious practices and also their culinary ones. The Hindu tendency towards abstention from meat, onion and garlic was enhanced (these foods all being hallmarks of Muslim cuisine). Common foods for Delhi's Hindu population remained much the same as they had beem before the Muslim invasion: *rice* and *pulses cooked together, millet, green leafy vegetables, gourds, sugar, ghee, sesame seeds*. High-born Hindus did not, as a rule, drink alcohol, but lower-caste Hindus would have partaken of *local brews* made from rice, fruit and flowers.

Delhi's early Muslim population had little inclination towards living or working in the countryside but Hindus from the villages surrounding Delhi did take up work opportunities in the city, typically in lowly paid domestic positions such as cooks. An influential noble of the Lodi Sultans was so pleased with a 'dish of tasty greens' prepared by a Hindu cook that he rewarded her with a plate of gold coins. Long before the Muslims fashioned Delhi as their own, the local Hindu population had been enjoying the leafy green tops of mustard plants and radishes cooked with spices. Most commonly referred to as saag, you will find it on menus all over Delhi (**Sweets Corner** does a good version). You might also like to have a recipe for saag—it's easy to prepare and a delicious way to eat your greens.

■ *Saag* ■
Serves 4

Saag is traditionally made with the green tops of mustard plants or other green leafy vegetables. Spinach is probably the most easily available vegetable to make it with though. You could also use a mixture of greens.

Ingredients
1 kg spinach (or other greens)
$^1/_2$ cup oil

50 g ghee or butter
2 onions, finely chopped
$^1/_2$ tsp fennel seeds, crushed
3 whole green cardamom pods, crushed
1-cm piece ginger grated or chopped
salt and pepper to taste

Method

Wash spinach thoroughly. Drain and chop fine.

Heat oil and ghee or butter in pan and fry onions until translucent.

Add spinach, spice powders, ginger and salt. Cover and cook over medium heat for 10 minutes, stirring occasionally.

Remove lid and cook until there is only a little liquid in the pan.

Stir in pepper and serve.

At the final step you can also blend the saag in a blender to create a smooth purée.

If you want to recreate the ancient Hindu version of this dish, leave out the onions, add a pinch of asafoetida and gently fry the spices in the oil/ghee. Then proceed as per the recipe.

In the late twelfth century a huge reservoir known as **Hauz Khas** was built to supply water to Delhi. A *madrasa* (college of Islamic instruction) was built on its shoreline. Unlike Hindu students who were expected to lead somewhat austere lifestyles, the young Muslim students here dined in the college canteen in a sumptuous fashion. '*Pheasant, partridge, herons, fish, roasted fowl, grilled kids, fried loaves, brightly coloured sweets of different kinds and other good things were heaped everywhere in large quantities*'. Pomegranate syrup was drunk and betel nuts served at the end of the meal. When the water receded in the drier months the banks of Hauz Khas reservoir were used to grow sugar cane, gherkins, cucumbers and small, sweet, green and yellow melons. This recipe for curried partridge, however, is unlikely to appear on many college menus today!

■ *Curried Patridge (Titar)* ■
Serves 6

Ingredients
6 partridge or any other game bird (about 600 g)
the hearts, livers and gizzards of the above
3 tsp salt
$^1/_2$ cup lime juice
1 tsp cumin seeds
seeds of 2 black cardamoms
8 cloves
3-cm stick cinnamon
4 tbsp ghee
2 onions, finely sliced
3 cloves garlic, chopped
5-cm piece ginger, finely grated
1 tsp turmeric powder
$^1/_2$ tsp freshly ground black pepper
4 tbsp curd

Method
Wash birds and pat dry with kitchen paper. Chop livers, hearts, gizzards and set aside. Rub birds with salt inside and outside. Place in a tray and sprinkle with lime juice.

Roast cumin, cardamom, cloves and cinnamon and grind.

Heat ghee and fry onions until crisp and golden. Remove from ghee and drain on kitchen paper. Add garlic and ginger to ghee and fry until slightly softened. Add livers etc. Cook until lightly browned. Add turmeric, roasted ground spices and black pepper. Fry for a few minutes, then remove from heat and add curd. Mix well.

Smear partridges, inside and out with this paste and leave them to marinate for at least 8 hours at room temperature.

To cook: place birds on a rack over a baking tray. Spoon any marinade over them. Pour boiling water into baking tray to come about half way up the tray. Bake in moderate oven (preheated to 180°C) for about 45 minutes, basting occasionally. Let them rest for 10 minutes before serving.

Hauz Khas is today a large park and the ruins of the madrasa still stand on the now waterless shore. Hauz Khas is also a smart shopping village full of exclusive boutiques and fashionable restaurants. If you climb the long staircase of the Village Bistro complex you will find yourself in the open-air **Top of the Village** restaurant. If you dine here at night the ruins are floodlit and very atmospheric. During the day you can look southwards and enjoy a panoramic view over the area where the cities of the Sultanate stood. The predominantly tandoori food served here bears little historical relationship to the food of the Delhi Sultans, but the setting allows one the scope to imagine how Delhi might have been in that period.

The Delhi Sultans ruled for four and a half centuries—between 1191 and 1526—but they are often historically overshadowed by the glamorous excesses of Delhi's Mughal rule. The reign of the Sultans is, however, one of the most significant periods of Delhi's development. Unlike the Mughals whose affections for cities constantly wavered, the Sultans remained loyal to Delhi and it was their capital throughout their entire reign (though there was one brief hiatus in 1332 when, on the whim of Muhammad bin Tughlaq, Delhi was abandoned and the capital moved to Daulatabad in Maharashtra). Under Sultan sovereignty, Delhi grew to be a city proper, of 'vast extent and population' (Sultanate Delhi was actually made up of four interconnecting cities: Delhi, Siri, Jahanpanah and Tughlaqabad). It was also the period when the foundations were laid for the cuisine that the Mughals later took to great heights and which became the cuisine that much of the world recognizes as 'Indian food'.

The glory of the Sultan's Muslim metropolis had not gone unnoticed, and throughout their rule they were continually engaged in fending off attacks from ambitious rivals eager to gain the prize of such a city. Ambition also ran high within the Sultanate itself and the final century of their rule saw them as heavily embroiled in the quagmire of internal power games as the Rajputs had been when the Sultans took the city from them. Weakened by both constant external vigilance and internal instability, their grip on the city became increasingly tenuous and the inevitable conclusion of the Sultanate era came in April 1526 when the Mughals captured Delhi.

OLD AND FAMOUS JALEBIWALA
1795 Dariba Kalan
Chandni Chowk
9 a.m.-10 p.m.

PANCHAYAT
92, N.D.M.C. Market
Connaught Circus
23414644, 23412596

PRINCE PAAN
M-29/2 Greater Kailash I
M-Block Market
26425052

SWEETS CORNER
1 Sunder Nagar Market
246119262
10 a.m.-11 p.m.

TOP OF THE VILLAGE
The Village Bistro
    Restaurant Complex
12 Hauz Khas Village
Tel: 26852227, 26853857
Internet: http://
fhrandia.com/restaurant/
delhi/bistro

■ Suggested tour

The scant remains of ancient Delhi are amply compensated for by the abundance of architecture that survives in the city from the Sultanate period: the World Heritage listed Qutab Minar, the haunting Tughlaqabad; Hauz Khas with its crumbling madrasa and tombs; Firoz Shah Kotla where djinns are worshipped and fed honey every Thursday; the tranquil Lodi Gardens and Hazrat Nizamuddin's dargah. Many of these sites are mere remnants of the cities they were once part of. Firoz Shah Kotla is now all that remains of Firozabad, which in the fourteenth century stretched from Hauz Khas in the south, north up to the Ridge and eastward to the Yamuna.

With the exception of Firoz Shah Kotla, all the Sultanate period sites are located reasonably close to one another in Delhi's south. Most visitors will have the

Qutab Minar at the top of their list, but Tughlaqabad and Nizamuddin's dargah are of equal merit. For best effect, when visiting these sites, you should provision yourself with some tastes from the Sultanate period (particularly if you visit Tughlaqabad, as it usually has no refreshment providers).

The food of the Sultanate era laid the groundwork for the later elaborate Mughal food that you will best enjoy in Delhi's restaurants (see 'Suggested tour' in chapter 'Mughal Delhi'). What you need for your Sultanate explorations are some portable foods such as samosas and jalebis. Both these food items were introduced into Delhi in the Sultanate era and both have survived the journey into modern times with little alteration. A good sweet shop should be able to pack some up for you. Ideally samosas and jalebi should be hot but they will stand up well to transportation. A portable flask full of rose-flavoured sharbat is the perfect Sultanate accompaniment to these. Provisioned thus, you can begin your exploration of the Sultanate world accompanied by some significant tastes of that era.

If you visit Hazrat Nizamuddin's dargah there are several 'hotels' selling simple Muslim fare such as *kababs*, *mutton curry*, *sheermal*, *halwa* and *naan* (**Mehboob Hotel** outside the Buland Gate of the dargah is recommended). This is the same fare that the average Muslim citizen of the Sultanate era would have enjoyed. If these sparse and stark 'hotels' do not suit you, there is a branch of **Karim's** in Nizamuddin. The food served here is of Mughal pedigree but you can still acquit yourself well on some simple kababs and freshly baked bread (and pay considerably more than you would in one of the adjacent 'hotels').

As you wander the narrow lanes of Nizamuddin village you will also find several small bakery shops which (unfortunately for the employees of these enterprises) do not seem to have been updated since medieval times!

An exploration of Sultanate Delhi must be accompanied at some point by a paan. If you don't feel confident indiscriminately purchasing a paan from any street vendor then visit the paan shops suggested in this chapter.

Three

■

MUGHAL DELHI

■ Great Mughals 1526–1707

1526–1530 Babur
1530–1556 Humayun
1556–1605 Akbar
1605–1627 Jehangir
1627–1658 Shah Jahan
1658-1707 Aurangzeb

■ Later Mughals 1707–1857

Three days after he captured Delhi on 24 April 1526, Babur the Mughal formally proclaimed himself ruler of the city. Apart from sharing a religion (Islam) and an ancestral homeland (Central Asia), Babur had little in common with the Delhi Sultans and he had no qualms about brutally liberating them from their rule of Delhi. Unremitting conquest was in Babur's blood; he proudly traced his lineage back to the ruthless Mongol Ghengis Khan and to Timur Lang (Tamerlane). When Babur captured Delhi, he was literally following in the footsteps of one of his ancestors. Timur Lang had captured Delhi in 1398 but he had only stayed long enough to thoroughly raid and loot the city. Unlike Timur, when Babur came and captured Delhi, he came to stay. A minor ruler in his native Fergana, Babur's capture of Delhi elevated him to the position of Emperor of Hindustan. It was a short-lived reign. Babur died in 1530 but his four years of rule had been time enough to lay the foundations for the Mughal dynasty that was to rule Delhi and much of India for the next three hundred years. It was also the Mughal dynasty that shaped much of what is familiar to us as Indian architecture, art and food.

When one contemplates the perfect symmetry of the Taj Mahal, marvels at the intricacies of a precious Mughal miniature painting, or when one sighs with satisfaction at the taste of a Mughlai dish, it is hard to imagine that the artistically inclined Mughal dynasty was once considered barbaric philistines. In the early decades of their rule, the Mughals were admired only for their martial skills and the fierce determination that had enabled them to so quickly rule much of northern India. There was little sign of the creative effervescence that would later come through. Babur's daughter, Gulbadan Begum, writes of her royal person being welcomed to Delhi with a rustic feast of *roasted sheep*, *bread* and *fruit*. It would take time and money for the Mughals to fully develop their artistic sensibilities.

Like the Sultans, the Mughals were relatively recent converts to Islam but they lacked the pious conviction of the Sultans. The Delhi Sultans had been intent on creating a great Islamic power base in India but the Mughals were interested in creating an empire to glorify themselves. The Sultan's piety was perhaps driven by their desire to make up for their low-class roots but the Mughals had no such doubts about themselves. Proud of their relationship to two of Asia's most feared subjugators, they were fuelled by a desire to continue the family business of enforced acquisition. As the Mughals conquered more and more of India, they began to accumulate enormous power and wealth. Once their rule was reasonably secured (always at best a tentative proposition in Medieval India), the Mughals, in typical nouveau riche style, began to live a lifestyle of ostentatious decadence. The shimmering brilliance of a mating peacock's tail was no match for the finery with which the Mughal Emperors began to adorn themselves and their palaces. Once they started there was no limit as to what the Mughals would spend to create the image of themselves that they believed was fitting—that of Gods on earth.

This heady consumerism extended to culinary matters and the Mughals garnished their food with thinly beaten sheets of gold and silver. European visitors to their courts recounted being served over fifty different dishes at a meal. The Mughal Emperor Akbar made the grandiose claim in his journal that he felt no meal was complete without five hundred dishes. Like all Muslims, the Mughals would not eat pork but they put few other limitations on flesh eating and they had a particular penchant for *wild game*, *ducks* and *waterfowl*. They liked their food cooked liberally in *ghee* and generous measures of *nuts* and both *fresh and dried fruits* were used in both sweet and savoury dishes. A variety of *wheat breads* accompanied meals and *rice* was cooked with *meat*, *spices* and *curd* to produce elaborate *biryani* and *pulao*. The Mughals also enjoyed meat cooked with wheat in dishes such as *haleem* (see 'Festivals' chapter for recipe). An extensive selection of prepared sweets and fruit were always served as a final course. Paan would be offered at the end of the meal and sometimes *tea* in china cups was served (tea was an expensive and exotic drink at this time; it was not yet grown in India and was imported from China).

The richness of the food was matched by the opulence of the Mughal table. Food was served on gold and silver dishes and the Emperor ate out of jade plates imported from China that changed colour if they came in contact with any of the common poisons of the time. (Poisoning was a popular way to get rid of enemies and food tasters were employed as a safety measure. These 'tasters' and royal cooks could often be bribed though, and Babur was very nearly poisoned when the mother of the recently deposed Sultan bribed Babur's cook.) Dishes were sealed on their way from the kitchen to the palace dining hall to prevent any contamination, and the bearded Muslim cooks wore gauze masks over their beards to prevent any hair from falling into the food. Drinking cups were often carved from jade or cast in gold and inlaid with precious stones. Meals were taken reclining on the floor and a large sheet of leather covered with layers of pure white calico cloth was laid down before meals to protect the elaborate carpets that lined the Mughal palaces. A second set of clean sheets was laid down before the sweetmeats and fruits were served. It almost goes without saying that there was a large retinue of servants standing by to respond to the Emperor's every command.

The Mughals' ancestors had been nomads as well as warriors and unable to resist the urges of their nomadic roots, the Mughals were always on the move. When they were not off fighting wars with rival Indian states, they were seeking relief from the summer swelter of the Indian plains in the cooler climates of Kashmir, Samarkand and Kabul. In 1556, the Mughal Emperor Akbar moved the capital from Delhi to Agra, and in 1638 the Mughal Emperor Shah Jahan moved the capital back to Delhi. In the one hundred years since a relatively rustic Babur had conquered Delhi, his great great grandson, Shah Jahan, had become renowned for his flamboyant style and highly developed aesthetic sensibility. He had a particular passion for architecture and it is he who was responsible for the construction of the Taj Mahal. To indulge his passion for building further, Shah Jahan had a whole new city built in Delhi.

Shah Jahan's Delhi, Shahjahanabad, occupied a piece of land overlooking the Yamuna a few kilometres upriver from Firozabad (the former city of the Sultan Firoz Shah was left derelict after many of its buildings were demolished to provide building materials for Shahjahanabad). A horoscope had been drawn up for the city, and to ensure its auspicious prosperity, the city was laid out in the shape of an archer's bow. Several prisoners were beheaded and buried in the foundations of the new city to ensure that it had a soul (a criminal one no less!) Covering an area of seven miles, the city was surrounded by a thick stone wall and there were seven majestic gateways into the city. The axis of the city was the Imperial Palace (the Lal Qila or Red Fort) and the Emperor the unchallengeable arbiter of the city's tastes and style. Those who could afford to, emulated the refinements of the court. Within the high walls, an extraordinary city developed full of bustling markets, splendid mansions, lush gardens and towering minarets. The wide boulevard of Chandni Chowk dissected the city, and down its entire length ran a canal that terminated within the walls of the palace where it fed the many fountains that spouted in the imperial household. Poets, writers and craftsmen were nurtured there and the city exuded cultural finesse. Such was the splendour of

Shahjahanabad, that the poet Amir Khusrau proclaimed: 'If there is a paradise on the face of the earth, it is this, it is this, it is this.' Shahjahanabad is the area of Delhi that is today called **Purani Dilli** or Old Delhi.

The Mughal economic system differed little from that of the Sultans. The Hindu peasants tilled the land and its revenues were drawn as taxes by the Emperor. The power of the Emperor was absolute; all the land ruled over by the Emperor was crown land and he was the ultimate owner of all property. On death, all a person's assets reverted to the Emperor so there was no incentive to accumulate as nothing could be passed on to family members. Unable to ensure the security of future generations, those who had any money made sure that they spent it on worldly pleasures. Fuelled by this enforced reckless attitude and the enormous wealth accumulated in the imperial coffers—with which the Emperor lavishly endowed his court—the Mughal era in the newly built Delhi was one of wild ostentation. Leading the way in such excesses, Shah Jahan would routinely crush precious gems into his wine as an aphrodisiac.

Francois Bernier was a French physician who spent several years in Delhi during the reign of Emperor Aurangzeb in the service of one of his nobles. Bernier's erudite memoirs of his sojourn in Delhi offer us details of daily life in the city that the court chronicles find no room for. Bernier's Delhi is not the entirely splendid city of Mughal grandeur. He does record the palatial mansions and palaces of Delhi's elite but says that these are surrounded by 'wretched mud and thatch huts which appeared less a town than a collection of many villages'. He also tells us that there is great poverty and that 'seven out of ten people are very badly dressed'. The absolute inequality of the Mughal economic system meant that all the splendour and glory was really only available to the privileged members of the Mughal court. While the members of that court dined daily on a multitude of elaborately prepared and presented dishes, the average Muslim citizen dwelling within Delhi's walled confines ate much humbler fare such as *keema, naan, kababs* and *sweet rice dishes*—essentially the same daily fare that their counterparts in the Sultanate era had eaten and the same dishes that are still sold in the food stalls and restaurants that surround the Jama Masjid in Old Delhi.

■ *Keema Matar* ■
Serves 6

Ingredients
2 tbsp oil
2 onions, finely chopped
8 cloves of garlic, crushed
1 tbsp ginger, minced
salt to taste
1 tsp red chilli powder (or to taste)
1 tsp ground coriander seeds

1 tsp ground cumin
1 tsp garam masala powder
2 green chillies, seeded and chopped
1 kg minced mutton
1 cup shelled green peas
1 $^1/_2$ tbsp lime juice

Method

Heat oil in a heavy-based frying pan and add onions, garlic, ginger and salt and cook until lightly browned.

Add spice powders and green chillies. Mix through onions and add mince. Stir for 5 minutes breaking up any lumps. Add $^3/_4$ cup hot water, bring to boil, cover pan, lower heat and simmer for 30 minutes.

Add peas and lime juice. Cook until liquid has been reduced. Adjust seasoning if necessary. Serve hot or cold.

■ *Seekh Kabab* ■
Makes 12 pieces

Ingredients

1 kg minced mutton
$^1/_4$ cup ghee
$^1/_4$ onion, minced
$^1/_4$ cup minced ginger
2 green chillies, minced
$^1/_3$ cup finely chopped fresh coriander
$^1/_3$ cup almonds, finely chopped
2 eggs, lightly beaten
$^1/_2$ tsp ground white pepper
2 tsp garam masala powder
salt to taste
metal or wooden skewers (if using wooden soak them in
water for $^1/_2$ hour before use)

Method

Mix all ingredients together until thoroughly blended and set aside for 15 minutes. Divide mixture into 12 even portions.

With wet hands shape each portion around a skewer by pressing the mince along the length of the skewer into a long sausage.

Cook over a charcoal grill, turning to ensure even cooking. You could also place them in a tray and cook them in an oven preheated to 180°C for 20 minutes).

European Influence

By the mid-seventeenth century, Europeans were making their way to Delhi either to seek dispensation of trading rights from the Mughal Emperor or to see for themselves the wondrous city that had long been the subject of myth making. Their subsequent reportage illuminated life in imperial Delhi for their countrymen and it also created its own myths.

The dynastic title of 'Mughal' is not the nomenclature that the inhabitants of Shah Jahan's Delhi would have known Babur and his ruling descendants by. Rather they called them 'Timurid' to denote their descent from Timur. Mughal is a variation of 'Mongol' which was used in northern India to distinguish immigrants from the local Muslims. When Europeans began to visit Delhi they mistakenly thought that 'Mongol'—which they spelt 'Mughal'—was applied exclusively to the ruling descendants of Babur. They used the term 'Mughal' when referring to Delhi's rulers in their reports home and the name gained currency in Europe and the European-bestowed 'Mughal' became the accepted name of this dynasty.

The arrival of Europeans in Delhi also created a culinary myth. The Mughals are often attributed with introducing *kababs, almonds, rosewater, pulao* and *flesh and fruit cooked together* to Indian cuisine, yet these same foods had long been enjoyed in the courts of the Delhi Sultanate. Europeans only began to visit Delhi during the Mughal era, and as they had little knowledge of the Sultanate period, they ascribed the cuisine they found the Mughals eating, to them (the egocentric Mughals would have made no attempts to dispel this notion). What the Mughals can be acknowledged for is the development and refinement of the dishes of the Sultans; and it was the Europeans who brought to their courts many of the foods that enabled them to achieve their culinary glory. It is hard to imagine Indian food without chilli, eggplant, corn, coriander, peanuts, cashew nuts, red kidney beans, guava, pepper, tomatoes and potatoes, but these foods from the New World did not enter Indian culinary life until Europeans started to visit India. The Mughals were quick to develop these new foods, adding them to already familiar dishes and creating new ones based on them. They also encouraged their cultivation, and as the native climate of these plant foods was not dissimilar to that of India, they flourished in the rich soil. Chillies in particular grew well and easily and very soon they began replacing or being used in addition to indigenous black pepper.

Apart from contributing new foods to the cuisine of Delhi, Europeans also inadvertently contributed to the development of the restaurant business in the city and to the predominance of Mughlai dishes on Indian restaurant menus the world over. The culinary extravagance of the Mughal court and the emulation of that extravagance by the princes, nobles and wealthy households of Delhi ensured plenty of employment for cooks. Cooking was a hereditary profession and generations of the same families passed through the kitchens of these elevated households. Recipes and techniques were handed down from father to son (women would have done the cooking in the home but men were the ones employed as cooks) and usually remained carefully guarded family secrets. After the death of the last Great Mughal, Aurangzeb, in 1707, the glorious Mughal empire began a slow decline. The tail-end of Mughal rule had not been august, but a royal court had remained where cooks could still gain employment. After the events of the 1857 Mutiny, the British seized control of Delhi, exiled the last Mughal Emperor to Burma and banned Muslims from the city. Delhi's imperial cooks not only lost their employer but their home as well.

Many of these exiled cooks—and their descendants— were eventually able to return to Delhi, but there was no imperial court in which they could apply their skills. They had to do something to create employment for themselves (cooking was their hereditary profession and the strictures of the Indian 'guild' system meant that it was not possible to take up something else). One possible choice for these former royal cooks was to sell their food to Delhi's citizens. The distinctive cuisine that had been eaten in the royal courts soon became available to the public and a motion was set in progress that saw Mughlai food develop into the restaurant food that people all over the world recognize as 'Indian food': *naan, skewered meats, pulao, biryani, meat and vegetables in rich, heavily spiced curries*, and *cloying sweets*. Regrettably, the Mughlai food served in many restaurants—both in Delhi and around the world—has been standardized and bastardized into something that only vaguely resembles its parent dish. This makes it an even greater pleasure to taste food that is a loyal version of the original.

There is no restaurant in Delhi with such an impressive Mughal pedigree as **Karim's**. A Delhi institution, Karim's has been operating since 1913 but the restaurant's origins can be traced all the way back to the first Mughal Emperor, Babur. The forefather of Karim's founder was a Saudi Arabian soldier who had come to India in the early 1500s to seek his fortune. He gained employment in the army of Babur where his talent as a cook soon outshone his martial abilities and he eventually became Babur's personal cook; fortune had smiled upon him and a lineage of imperial cooks was born. Three centuries later when the

British exiled all the Muslims from the city of Delhi, the descendants of Babur's personal cook went into hiding at Ghaziabad, not returning to the city until 1911. The occasion of the family's return was the coronation of George V. The head of the family, Haji Karimuddin, set up a small street stall selling *chapatis*, *aloo gosht* and *dal* to the crowds that had gathered in Delhi for the celebrations. Haji Karimuddin was more specific in his claims on providence than his ancestor had been, proclaiming, 'I want to earn fame and money by serving royal food to the common man.' Two years later he had opened Karim's restaurant on the site where it still operates today (the branch in Old Delhi).

To find Karim's you walk down **Bazaar Matya Mahal**, which lies adjacent to the south gate of the **Jama Masjid**. You will know you are in the right place from the shops piled high with wheat-coloured *sevian* (vermicelli) and the neat rows of squatting Muslim beggars waiting patiently outside the small restaurants or 'hotels' to be given a meal by some more fortunate patron. Or you can ask anyone you meet on the way—everyone knows where the famous Karim's restaurant is. Turn left into the first narrow laneway, **Gali Kabab**, and follow your nose down this short lane until it opens into a spotless courtyard bustling with activity. All the surrounding buildings are Karim's kitchens and dining rooms. Peek into any of the doorways or windows and you will see some facet of Karim's in operation: a strong-armed chef carefully stirring a pot of delicate *nehari*; a young apprentice shaping kababs onto thin metal skewers while another cooks them over glowing coals; dining rooms humming with busy waiters and eager patrons.

Karim's is a family business and the family closely guards the recipes on which its reputation has been made. Each morning the cooks have to place orders for the masala that they will need for that day's cooking. The masalas are then freshly ground by immediate family members and sent in a box to the restaurant cooks. The recipes used at Karim's are family heirlooms and they have come to the present family members via the courts of the Mughals. This is the food that the Mughal Emperors would have eaten except that the food of the Emperors was rich with calorie-laden ghee and the food at Karim's is now cooked in vegetable oil to satisfy the changing preferences and health concerns of modern patrons.

There is a preponderance of meat dishes on the menu at Karim's. Vegetarians are catered for, but this is the place to go for a carnivorous feast. Muslims in general are very fond of meat, but the flesh of animals in India is often very lean and it has rarely been regarded for its tenderness. To counter this, Muslim cooks became experts at tenderizing meat. This was very important for royal cooks as there was no question that the Emperor should be inconvenienced by a tough piece of meat. In the process, many distinctive dishes were created. To sample this art of tenderizing, order the satin-smooth *Shahjahan kabab*, the velvet-soft *Akbari murgh masala* (chicken tenderized with curd and spices) or the supple *Badshahi badam pasanda*. Pasanda (or parsinda) is a traditional Delhi cut of meat taken from the shoulder or leg, cut into small pieces and then flattened or scored with a knife.

■ *Sookhe Parsinde* ■
From *The Essential Delhi Cookbook*
Seves 10-12

Ingredients
200 g garlic
5-cm piece ginger
4 tbsp lime juice
1 $1/2$ tsp salt
a pinch of red chilli powder
2 kg parsindas
$3^1/2$ tsp poppy seeds (khus-khus)
180 g chironji (substitute pine nuts if need be)
500 g curd
2 tbsp ghee
lime wedges and onion rings to garnish

Method
Grind garlic and ginger, mix in lime juice, salt and chilli powder. Rub well over meat. Leave to marinate for at least 4 hours.

Roast poppy seeds and chironji on tava or griddle. Grind and mix into meat along with curd and ghee. Put into a shallow baking dish and cook in an oven preheated to 400°F (200°C) for $1^1/2$ hours. Reduce heat to 350°F (180°C) and cook for one hour more or till tender. Turn meat once or twice during baking.

Serve garnished with lime wedges and onion rings.

For the offal connoisseur, *nayab magaz masala* (mutton brain curry) is an essential at Karim's. Karim's is also the place to enjoy a plate of steaming hot nehari. Nehari is a stew that is traditionally made overnight and eaten for breakfast ('nehari' means 'dawn'). Typically made from sheep's trotters or knuckles or a goat's head, it is considered to be very nourishing and a source of great energy. It was this dish that the Mughal armies marched on. (Given their Emperors' love of warring it was essential that the Mughal army be kept in good form!) There was no question of soldiers enjoying the refined dishes of their masters but it was vital to ensure that the soldiers were kept robust with nutritious food. After getting up well before sunrise to complete training exercises, the soldiers started their day with a hearty meal of nehari. Eating nehari was not exclusive to the army though, and it was a dish that Delhi's civilian population also enjoyed.

In Old Delhi it is still traditional to eat nehari for breakfast particularly on the weekends. To cater to the wide vagaries of modern taste, different types of nehari are served. Some are made only with mutton (no trotters) and some versions are heavily spiced but free of chilli. If you feel up to starting your day with the dish that an imperial army once marched on, visit Karim's early in the morning or try **Hotel Flora**. Both these places are in the Jama Masjid area. Go early and enjoy the gusto with which the locals enjoy this substantial breakfast after their morning prayers. During the Muslim month of Ramadan, when it is incumbent on the faithful not to eat or drink during daylight hours, nehari is a favourite dish with which to break the fast.

■ *Paye ki Nehari* ■
From *The Essential Delhi Cookbook*
Serves 4-5

Ingredients
2 pairs sheep's trotters
3 medium onions
25 cloves garlic
3 tsp coriander seeds
2 dried red chillies
1 tsp salt
$^1/_2$ tsp turmeric powder
$^3/_4$ cup ghee
$1^1/_2$ cups curd, beaten smooth with a fork
2-3 green chillies, chopped
2 tbsp chopped fresh coriander leaves
6 cloves
1 tsp garam masala powder (see below)

Method
Put trotters into boiling water and clean thoroughly. Cut into pieces (or have the butcher do it for you).

Grind onions, garlic, coriander seeds and red chillies. Mix in salt and turmeric. Heat $^1/_2$ cup ghee in a pressure cooker* and fry masala paste for 2-3 minutes. Put in trotters and $3^3/_4$ cups water and cook under pressure for 45 minutes.

Allow pressure to drop by itself. Cool slightly, then remove trotters. Using a marrow-spoon, take out all the marrow and stir into cooking liquid. Discard bones.

Stir and cook nehari for 5-10 minutes. Add whipped curd, green chillies and coriander leaves. Heat remaining ghee in a small pan, fry cloves and add to the nehari with garam masala.

*The use of a pressure cooker is a modern adaptation. If you wish to follow a more traditional method put the trotters in a large pan, cover with plenty of water and cook on low heat for 4-5 hours. (Keep checking during cooking and add more water if necessary.) Cool and proceed as above.

■ *Garam masala powder* ■

Ingredients
3 tsp black peppercorns
3 tsp cumin seeds
20 cloves
5 bay leaves, crushed
a good pinch of mace flakes
seeds of 5 black cardamoms
seeds of 20 green cardamoms
3 x 3-cm sticks cinnamon
1 nutmeg

Method
Separately roast the first 5 ingredients on a hot griddle. Cool and grind with cardamom seeds, cinnamon and nutmeg (these are not roasted as they become bitter). Sieve and store in an airtight container.

You can also easily buy ready-made garam masala powder but freshly made is always better.

Despite the prospect of dining on superb food, many Delhiites were not keen on crossing town to eat at Karim's in Old Delhi (seen through the romantic eyes of the newcomer, the area is fascinating, but to the local it is often just frustrating and squalid). To capture this eager-to-eat-but-unwilling-to-be-inconvenienced market, the Karim's family opened a second restaurant, **Dastarkhan-e-Karim** in Nizamuddin in 1974. The food remains essentially the same here but the decor and atmosphere are distinctly upmarket. Here the whitewashed austerity of the Old Delhi premises gives way to a den of soothing blues and greens, wood-panelled walls and silver water jugs and finger bowls—a veritable oasis in the middle of bustling Nizamuddin village.

The proprietors of Karim's believe that they owe their success to the 'grace of Allah' and there is no compromising religious ethics here. Alcohol is strictly banned and this view is so strongly upheld that the family chose to close down a Mumbai branch of the restaurant rather than serve liquor there.

When the British exiled the Muslims from Delhi, a number of royal cooks fled to the Muslims cities of Hyderabad and Lucknow where they were eagerly employed by the local Nawabs who were keen to use the skills of these Delhi-trained cooks to enrich their own cuisines. The Nawab of Awadh (Lucknow) was an enthusiastic gourmet and he welcomed not only Mughal influence into his kitchens but also that of the British. The Awadhi cuisine that developed under these influences took the richness of Mughal food and added to it the *cream*, *roux* (flour and fat paste used as a thickener), *refined gravies* and *alcohol* of European cooking. These rich dishes were often cooked in the *dumpukht* style where a dish is covered with a seal of pastry and left to cook within. The pastry cap seals in the flavours and moisture of the food and leaves it delicate and tender. You can dine on royal Awadhi cuisine in Delhi at the aptly named **Dum Pukht**. This is one of Delhi's best restaurants, the surroundings are extravagant—Wedgwood-blue walls, chandeliers, heavily patterned furnishings—and the food exquisite. The *jhinga dum nisha* (prawns cooked dumpukht style) is a must. The kitchens of the Awadhi Nawab are also credited with creating the famous *kakori kabab*. Tender and fragile, these delectable discs of gently spiced meat were said to have been prepared for the Nawab whose lifetime of gormandizing had left his teeth in such bad shape that he could not chew. An alternative theory says that kakori kababs were inspired by a European who complained that the meat served to him by the Nawab was tough. Insulted, the Nawab determined to present this European gentleman with the most tender and delicate piece of meat possible. You can order kakori kabab at Dum Pukht or you might like to visit **Al Kauser** where Dilliwallahs pull up late into evening to enjoy them kerbside in their cars or take them home for private consumption.

City of Sweets

With its wide expanses bisected by the central canal, parallel rows of luxuriant shade-giving trees and a magnificent caravanserai surrounded by splendid gardens (the British later replaced this opulent wonder with a pragmatic town hall), **Chandni Chowk** was a boulevard of exalted proportions during the Mughal era. It was also a dynamic marketplace full of all sorts of exquisite and expensive items. Amongst the dealers of gems, gold and silver ware, silks, fine carpets and fancy trinkets were to be found many sweet sellers. The giving and receiving of sweets was an important social ritual in Mughal Delhi. Merchants offered sweetmeats to their clients to nibble on while they engaged in rigorous haggling and no gracious home would have failed to offer sweets to guests. Traditional Delhi sweetmeats are made from ground nuts, pulses, sugar and fruit and there is much finesse involved in shaping these basic elements into delicate confections. Delhiites, both past and present, have always considered it best to leave the creation of their beloved sweets to the experts. Even the Emperor, with his well-appointed kitchens full of talented cooks, would visit Chandni Chowk to eat sweets.

While its ample proportions have been narrowed by 'efficient' British engineering and the dealers in luxury goods replaced by peddlers of more pedestrian items, Chandni Chowk still boasts many thriving sweet sellers. **Ghantewala** has been selling sweets in Chandni Chowk since 1790 and one of Delhi's later Emperors was in the habit of stopping there whenever he passed by on his favourite elephant. As a reward for faithful service, the pachyderm was always given a sweet treat on these stops. Legend has it that driven by an irresistible longing for these sweets, the elephant managed to make his own way to Ghantewala and wouldn't budge until he had his fill of sweets. When anyone tried to move him he shook his head and the bells strung around his neck would ring. That is suuposedly how the shop acquired its name (Ghantewala meaning 'bell ringer'). A less romantic explanation of the name is that the shop owner or one of his assistants would stand out at the front and ring a bell to attract customers. You won't encounter any bell ringers—animal or otherwise—at Ghantewala today but you will find authentic Delhi sweets there. Ghantewala sweets are made with best quality ingredients and are consequently relatively expensive but are worth every rupee. Sweets such as *piste ki lauz* (pistachio sweet), *badam ki lauz* (almond sweet) or *sohan halwa* (dried fruit, ground pulses and sugar) will give you a taste of Mughal Delhi and a taste of the art of master confectioners.

The most famous Delhi confection is *kulfi*, a frozen milk dessert flavoured with kewra, almonds or pistachios, cardamom and sometimes saffron. It derives its name from the distinctive conical mould that it is set in. Said to have been devised in the kitchens of the Mughal court, its creation was made possible by the boat-load of ice that arrived in Delhi everyday from the mountains near Kasauli. Although Delhi lays claim to kulfi as its own, it is likely that it originally evolved in the cooler climates of the mountain regions of Persia or Samarkand and that the Mughals appropriated the concept and elaborated on it to create the creamy, perfumed dessert that it now is. The English food writer Elizabeth David in her book *Harvest of the Cold Months* suggest that the kulfi mould may have been copied from seventeenth-century European bombe moulds or that conversely European bombe moulds may have been influenced by the kulfi moulds that Europeans had seen in Delhi. Akbar mentions the kulfi in his sixteenth-century journals and he introduced to India the saltpetre that was originally used for freezing kulfi—so the Indian influence on the European design seems more likely.

The kulfi vendor with his earthenware *baraf-ki-handi* (pot of ice) has been a Delhi tradition for centuries. The vendor himself probably descends from a long line of kulfiwallahs and is still a common sight in Old Delhi. Kulfi has become an inevitable inclusion on menus in Delhi and while restaurants now use modern freezing equipment, street vendors still use the method introduced by Akbar to freeze their sweets. The conical moulds (traditionally stoppered with dough) are placed into a terracotta pot filled with ice and salt and gently agitated until the kulfi freezes. The kulfi is kept cold in this portable 'freezer' and is served on a disposable plate constructed of dried leaves.

Kulfi is traditionally partnered with *falooda* (vermicelli noodles cooked with milk and sugar, perfumed with rose water and served cold). Falooda was taken as a beverage by the Mughals and was made by pressing the strainings of boiled wheat through a sieve to produce a starchy, jelly-like noodle. These noodles were then mixed with cream and fruit juices. In its modern form, falooda is made with sevian (the vermicelli-style wheat noodles that you see piled up for sale around Old Delhi) and it makes a delightfully slippery counterpart to the solid richness of the kulfi. **Roshan di Kulfi** are the best-known purveyors of kulfi in Delhi. It is a rare customer who can resist ordering the *kulfi kesar pista badam* (kulfi with saffron, almond and pistachio) after a meal. It comes partnered with a generous serve of falooda (for the novice—you tackle kulfi-falooda with two spoons much as you would use a spoon and fork to eat spaghetti). There is also **Gianiji ka Falooda** in Old Delhi which is considered by some aficionados to make the best kulfi-falooda in town (they have been at it since 1947). If the temptation of a creamy, ice-cold kulfi is not enough to get you onto the frenzied streets of Old Delhi or Karol Bagh, or if you are nowhere near either, then you can make it yourself.

■ *Kulfi* ■
Serves 4

Ingredients
4 cups full cream milk
$^1/_2$ tsp crushed saffron strings
6 tbsp fine sugar
seeds of 2 green cardamoms, crushed
$^1/_4$ cup slivered almonds
2 tbsp finely sliced pistachios nuts

Method
Boil milk over medium heat until it is reduced to half its original quantity.

Add saffron to milk while it is boiling.

Add sugar and boil for another 10 minutes. Remove from heat.

Add cardamom and nuts.

Divide mixture between 4 kulfi moulds or other appropriate containers (such as freezer trays or small dariole moulds). Cover any exposed surface with plastic wrap and freeze for 4 hours or until kulfi is set.

Unmould by dipping mould quickly in hot water and sliding out onto a plate. Serve plain or with falooda.

■ *Falooda* ■
Serves 4

Ingedients
1 cup cornflour
2 cups water
plenty of ice-cold water

Method

Mix corn flour and water and cook over low heat, stirring constantly until transparent. If required add a little more water.

Push the mixture through a fine metal colander, with the back of a spoon, into a large bowl of ice-cold water. Keep in refrigerator until required.

■ *Flavoured Milk* ■
Serves 4

Ingredients
2 cups milk
4 tbsp castor sugar
6 tbsp rose syrup (see recipe in chapter 'Sultanate Delhi')

Method

Bring milk to boil, add sugar and continue to boil until slightly reduced.

Add rose syrup and chill.

Add falooda to milk and re-chill.

Serve with kulfi.

When Babur first conquered Delhi, those who had accompanied him were not pleased about the prospect of permanent residency there—they had hoped to loot and leave. Accustomed to the temperate mountain regions of Samarkand, the inferno of the Indian plains was hard to bear. They were also homesick for the taste of the sweet fruits of their mountain provinces. To remedy this, Babur immediately set about importing *grapes* and *melons* (he did not like the small melons that he found growing on the banks of Hauz Khas). To speed their arrival for royal consumption, these fruits were often carried overland on platters by an ongoing chain of foot runners. Non-royals had to be content with the regular arrival of caravans laden with fruit from Samarkand, Kashmir, Kabul and Kandahar. The Mughals also put a lot of effort into growing fruit and encouraging its production in Delhi. Peasants who grew orchards of fruit could have their revenues remitted and owners of private gardens often rented them out to professional fruit growers and sellers. Melons and grapes thrived in the alluvial soil of Delhi's surrounding districts but other fruits such as apricots, cherries and pears had to continue to be imported from cooler areas. The *pineapples* that the Europeans brought to India from the New World were eagerly accepted and were soon cultivated in the palace gardens.

Bernier includes a long description of the variety of fruit available in Delhi in his memoir (this was at a time when most Europeans regarded fruit suspiciously and many of the varieties of fruit brought back from the New World to Europe were treated as ornamental and not edible):

There is indeed a fruit market that makes some show . . . in summer it is well supplied with dry fruit from Persia, Balk, Bokara (Bukhara) and Samarkand, such as almonds, pistachios and walnuts, raisins, prunes and apricots, and in winter with excellent fresh grapes, black and white brought from the same countries, wrapped in cotton; pears and apples of three or four sorts, and those admirable melons which last the whole winter. These fruits are however very dear; a single melon selling for a crown and a half.[1]

The Mughals also discovered some compensation for the Indian heat in the form of mangoes. They adored these luscious, sweet, juicy fruits of summer and encouraged the grafting of mango trees to create new varieties. The mangoes grown around Delhi were however considered 'indifferent' and the best ones came to the walled city from Mumbai and Goa. *Mulberry* (*shehthooth*) trees were imported from Persia by the Mughals and today you will still see people in Delhi enthusiastically gathering the fruit from these trees in the mulberry season (March/April). *Pomegranate* (*anar*) was also a favourite fruit and this unusual but simple soup was relished by the Mughals.

■ *Shorba-e-Anar (Pomegranate Soup)* ■
Serves 4-6

Ingredients
4 cups freshly pressed pomegranate juice
1 tbsp ground white pepper
1 tsp grated fresh ginger
1 tsp chilli powder
1 tsp roasted, ground cumin seeds
salt to taste

---

[1]Bernier, F., *Travels in the Mughal Empire* (London: Oxford University Press, 1916).

> 1 cup fresh spinach leaves (washed thoroughly
> to remove all dirt and grit)

Method

Bring pomegranate juice to a gentle boil.

Add all ingredients except spinach, give it a good stir and add spinach. Simmer over low heat for 5 minutes.

Serve hot or chilled.

It has been more than 150 years since a Mughal Emperor ruled over Delhi but the passion for fruit the Mughals instilled in the city remains. Baskets of fruit wrapped in brightly coloured cellophane are a highly esteemed gift in Delhi. Delhi fruit merchants can wrap a simple melon or a few apples and bananas in a fashion that rivals the packaging of even the most outlandish box of chocolates

Melons at Kinari Bazaar

(see chapter 'Where to Shop' for fruit sellers). Driving around Delhi you will see roadside fruitwallahs with stalls piled high with striped watermelons and carefully presented seasonal fruit set out in decorative patterns. Illuminated by the soft glow of a kerosene lantern in the evenings, these fruit stalls punctuate the roadside darkness beckoning like an irresistible Aladdin's cave.

Drinking in the Mughal Era

During the Mughal era Chandni Chowk was also home to numerous coffee houses. A Persian innovation, these coffee houses were popular gathering spots for men to drink *coffee*, listen to poetry, discuss literary and cultural matters and smoke *hookahs*. The popularity of drinking coffee must have been heightened by the Muslim restriction on alcohol. Bernier says that 'wine can be obtained in none of the shops in Delhi' and that the only available alcohol was *arrack*, a distilled liquor, which he warns wise men to avoid due to its harsh and potentially hazardous nature. He advises that the climate of Delhi is not conducive to wine-drinking and that *nimbu pani* is the most suitable drink.

Despite the prohibitions of their faith, the Mughal Emperors and their court relished wine, which they imported at great expense from Persia. Although grapes had been grown successfully around Delhi, the hot, humid climate made wine production difficult. The Emperor Jehangir was 'much addicted to wine' and drugs and he spent most of his reign in a hazy stupor. The exception to this was the zealous Emperor Aurangzeb. A teetotaller, he despised alcohol and he passed harsh prohibition laws in Delhi (though he permitted Christians to make and consume alcohol provided this was done a league from the walled city; also they were forbidden to sell it). Aurangzeb also dealt out harsh penalties to those caught breaking prohibition laws, but this had little effect on eliminating alcohol consumption and these laws quickly disappeared (he even tried to stop poorer people indulging in *charas*).

All the Mughal Emperors insisted on the use of water from the Ganga for their personal consumption; Yamuna water and rain water were sanctioned for cooking but a few drops of Ganga water were added to these to ensure purity. There was always a supply of auspicious Ganga water being ferried into Delhi and when the Emperor went on tour or to war, a special tent and bearers were employed solely for the provision of Ganga water to him.

Hindu-Muslim relations

The Mughals understood that to achieve consummate rule they would need to have an inclusive attitude to the Hindu population (which they maintained until the reign of the orthodox Aurangzeb whose doctrinal rigidity precipitated the demise of the Mughal empire). Not intellectually restricted by religious zealousness the Mughals were reasonably culturally fluid and they were eager to win over and please their Hindu subjects. They took numerous Hindu princesses into their harems and these high-born women soon showed their influence with Babur who swore to forgo beef, garlic and onions. Babur's grandson Akbar started his meals with *curd* and *rice*, a typically 'Indian' custom. He also practised almost total *vegetarianism* in an effort to appease his Hindu subjects. Although the Mughals willingly adopted some Hindu dietary habits, they certainly did not embrace the restrained Hindu attitude to food. What they most enjoyed eating remained the Persian-inspired dishes that formed the culinary legacy they had inherited and then enhanced, along with the city, from the Sultans.

While the Mughals encouraged the assimilation of Hindus, the majority of Delhi's Hindu population still preferred to live in villages outside the city walls. The land there was very fertile and *wheat, corn, sugar, rice, millet, pulses* and *indigo* were successfully cultivated. The Hindu population tilled the fields, raised crops and created the agricultural wealth that was squandered within the city walls. Most of the Hindu population did not share in the wealth they created and their simple village lifestyle continued unchanged. The rich food of the Mughal court had little impact on their dietary habits and they continued to eat as much as their ancestors had. The grains and pulses they grew along with vegetables such as *gourds* and *leafy* greens were still the mainstay of their diet, supplemented by the *milk* and related *dairy products* of their venerated cows and buffaloes. If meat was eaten it would have been *mutton* or the *wild game* that was then abundant around Delhi. Today this simple village life has changed little but the villages are no longer adjacent to the walls of the city; the sprawling morass of modern Delhi has pushed them out into the neighbouring states of Uttar Pradesh and Haryana—and there is no wild game to catch (and it is now illegal to do so).

Not all Hindus were content with simple village living though and life within the Mughal city walls beckoned the more aspirant educated castes. The Hindu Kayasths became the scribes of the Mughal court and their food became almost as rich as that of their employers. They adopted the Muslim passion for meat and married it with subtle Hindu spicing. The Hindu mercantile caste, the Banias, were attracted by the business opportunities in Shahjahanabad and they built up a solid and successful business community within the city walls. Originally from Rajasthan, their food habits had been established in ancient days and despite their presence in Delhi for several centuries, Bania food has never absorbed any Muslim or outside influences. Banias are strict vegetarians and onion and garlic are not eaten (asafoetida is commonly used instead). Bania food is always served on metal thalis as porcelain plates may contain animal bones.

Despite the Banias' considerable commercial influence in Delhi, you won't find Bania food readily served in restaurants in the city. The purity of the Bania kitchen is considered an essential part of its preparation and the demanding rituals required to achieve this purity have meant that it has remained a home food.

Lacking an invitation to a Bania home you might like to make this popular Bania dish, *kadhi*. The use of ground pulses made into balls and added to rice gruel or curds, or added to sauces to thicken them was well established in ancient India.

■ *Kadhi* ■
Serves 6
Dumplings:

Ingredients
1 cup gram flour (besan)
salt
$^1/_4$ tsp bicarbonate of soda (a modern addition, it makes
the batter light)
$^1/_2$ cup curd
vegetable oil or ghee for deep frying

Method
Sift gram flour into a bowl with salt and bicarbonate of soda.

Mix curd with a fork until smooth, add to flour mixture and beat until mixture is light and airy.

The batter should be thick but able to drop off a spoon, add more curd if necessary.

Put enough ghee or vegetable oil to come 2 cm up the side of a large frying pan and heat.

When hot, drop teaspoons of batter into the oil and cook until golden and cooked through.

Drain on absorbent paper towel.

Sauce:

Ingrdients
1 cup gram flour (besan)
2 cups curd
2 tbsp ghee or vegetable oil (ghee adds a more authentic flavour)
$^1/_4$ tsp asafoetida powder (hing)
$^1/_2$ tsp cumin seeds
$^1/_2$ tsp fenugreek seeds (methi)
$^1/_4$ tsp nigella seeds (kalonji)
3-4 whole dried red chillies
$^1/_4$ tsp turmeric powder
salt to taste

Method
Sift gram flour.

Whip curd with a fork until smooth and add to flour.

Stir in 5 cups water and mix. Add asafoetida. The sauce should be quite thin; add more water if necessary.

Heat oil or ghee and add cumin, fenugreek, nigella and chillies. Stir until chillies darken (this takes only seconds—keep an eye on it you do not want the chillies to burn).

Add gram flour mixture, turmeric and salt.

Stir constantly over medium heat until mixture thickens.

Add dumplings just before serving and cook for an further 10-15 minutes over low heat.

Serve with plain rice.

Banias are also renowned for their dishes made with vegetables such as yam, jackfruit and plantains.

■ *Kathal (Jackfruit) Curry* ■
Serves 4-5
From *The Essential Delhi Cookbook*

Ingredients
$1/2$ kg jackfruit (kathal)
1 cup ghee
a pinch of asafoetida powder (hing)
$1/2$ tsp cumin seeds
$1/2$ tsp turmeric powder
$1/2$ tsp red chilli powder
1 tsp coriander powder
1 tsp salt
2 medium tomatoes, chopped
$2/3$ cup (150 g) curd, beaten smooth with a fork
1 tsp garam masala powder (see Nehari recipe on p. 74)
$1/2$ tsp mango powder (amchur)

Method
Using greased hands and a greased knife, peel jackfruit and cut into 4-cm cubes.

Peel seeds, being careful to remove every bit of peel as it can make the dish bitter.

Heat ghee in a pan and fry jackfruit (not seeds) until golden. Drain and keep aside.

In the same ghee fry asafoetida and cumin for 1-2 minutes. Stir in turmeric, chilli powder, coriander, salt and tomatoes, and cook for 2-3 minutes. Add fried jackfruit, seeds and $1\,1/4$ cups water. Cover and cook on low heat for 30 minutes till jackfruit is tender. Add beaten curd, garam masala and mango powder. Cook for 10-15 minutes more.

Serve hot with rice or chapati.

GHANTEWALA
1862-A Chandni Chowk
23280404
10 a.m.-8.00 p.m.

DASTARKHWAN-E-KARIM
168/2 Hazrat Nizamuddin West
24968300, 24635458
Timings: 12.30 p.m.-
3.30 p.m. & 6.30 p.m.-
11.30 p.m. (Monday closed)

KARIM'S HOTELS
Jama Masjid Gate I
23269880, 23264981
7 a.m.-12 a.m.

HOTEL FLORA
4179 Urdu Bazar
Jama Masjid

DELHI KA AANGAN
Hyatt Regency
Bikaji Cama Place, Ring Road
26791234
12.00-3.00 p.m. &
7.00-12 p.m.

DUM PUKHT
ITC Maurya Sheraton Hotel
and Towers, Diplomatic
Enclave
Sardar Patel Marg
26112233
12.30-2.45 p.m. & 7.30-
11.40 p.m.

AL KAUSER
At the corner of Sadar Patel
and Kautliya Marg
Diplomatic Enclave
23015183, 23010427
6 p.m.-11 p.m.

ROSHAN DI KULFI
2816 Ajmal Khan Rd
Karol Bagh
25724230, 25782728
7 a.m.-10 p.m.

GIANIJI KA FALOODA
Fatehpuri Mosque
Chandni Chowk

■ Suggested tour

Delhi rose to its spectacular peak as a city in the seventeenth century when it took on a new form as the Mughal-built Shahjahanabad. Four centuries later, what remains of Shahjahanabad is now designated as Old Delhi and it is no longer a glittering prize. Much of Shah Jahan's urban paradise has been bulldozed, dismantled, left to rot or lost under modern edifices. It is also very congested; there are none of the wide open spaces of New Delhi here. Yet it remains a compelling—and at times frustrating—part of the city. Any exploration of Mughal Delhi would necessarily begin here and if your schedule permits, you may choose to make several visits to Old Delhi.

Those of hearty appetite might like to begin a 'Mughal' day with a plate of nehari at Karim's or Hotel Flora. Both these restaurants are in the Jama Masjid area; so after breakfast you can take a round of the *poultry* and *fish markets* on the south side of the mosque (the smell here can be a bit strong though, and you may not feel up to it first thing in the morning). After passing the market you can enter a park on your left and walk through it to Netaji Subhash Marg and across to the Mughal-built Lal Qila (Red Fort). If you prefer not to walk, you will find plenty of rickshawallahs milling around the area who will happily take you over to the fort for an inflated price. Try to walk, though, as it is the best way to really get a feel of the area, crowded and busy though it may be.

Lal Qila was the centrepiece of Shah Jahan's Delhi but I stress 'was'. Gone are the paradisiacal gardens criss-crossed with water channels, languid pools and gentle fountains. Gone are the decadent inlays of precious gems and metals in the walls and ceilings of the imperial buildings. Amir Khusrao's famous couplet could now read

'If there was paradise on earth, it *was* this, it *was* this, it *was* this.' The British used the fort as a military complex after they banished the last Muhgal Emperor in 1857 and they are often blamed for its demise. There can be no doubt that they did contribute significantly to its current state but the recollections of visitors to the fort prior to the British takeover indicate that it was already being neglected by its later Mughal keepers. Many of the buildings that remain in the complex (such as the bath house and the Pearl Mosque) are out of bounds. All that said, it is still worth visiting the fort; you can let the structural remains guide your imagination towards a vision of what life must have been like here during Shah Jahan's reign. There is also a small museum that houses, amongst its collection, examples of the 'Celadon' ware crockery that was used by the Mughal Emperors.

After you have finished at the fort it is time to visit Chandni Chowk. Sadly Chandni Chowk too is now a mere reminder of what it once was and the goods on offer are of a far more utilitarian nature than those that were sold there in the seventeenth century. Chandni Chowk retains some charms though; it is a living, breathing thoroughfare and along with its network of crooked, narrow lanes built with a special purpose, it is still the nerve centre of Delhi's Muslim population. (Old Delhi's narrow and maze-like streets, alleys and lanes were built to serve two purposes: the narrow lanes did not allow the searing North Indian sun in and the winding streets made it hard for invaders to penetrate them.)

Another of Chandni Chowk's charms is its guise as the street of sweets. As you make your way up Chandni Chowk from Lal Qila you will pass the Sikh temple, Gurudwara Sisganj. If you pay a visit to this busy Gurudwara you will be rewarded with your first sweet treat, a portion of the moorish *halwa* that is given to visitors as prasad. Continue onwards up Chandni Chowk to Old and Famous Jalebiwala for a jalebi; then continue on the same side of the street until you will find yourself at Ghantewala sweet shop. Try a few sweets here and then cross the road to the adjacent, very modern, **Haldiram's**. This perpetually busy sweetshop has a huge range of Indian sweets and an almost as vast selection of savoury snacks and drinks. You could spend hours here sampling, but leave room for a few paranthas in **Paranthe wale Gali**. (You can always pay a second visit to Ghantewala or Haldiram's on your journey back down the chowk.) As the name suggests, this gali is dedicated to the parantha and although these are technically of Punjabi origin, there is mention of paranthas in Mughal recipe books. You will need to cross back from Halidram's and continue up the street for a few hundred metres until you find Paranthe wale Gali (it's a very small lane which is easy to miss but a landmark is a small sweet shop on the corner of the lane). After you have had your fill of paranthas, come back onto Chandni Chowk. Don't forget to try the best *nimbu soda* in Delhi from the the **nimbuwallah** diagonally opposite the Town Hall (it is unlikely you will miss him because there is always a small crowd there).

Continue up to the western end of Chandni Chowk to the Fatehpuri Mosque and cross the road. Here you will find a number of kiosks in the arcade of the mosque selling *dry fruit and nuts*. This is the best place in Delhi to buy these; the quality is good, the prices competitive, and the merchants are happy for you to try a small sample before you buy. As you follow these stalls, to your right the fruit and nuts give way to colourful displays of both *whole and ground spices*. After passing several spice stalls you will eventually find your passage interrupted by a congestion of overloaded coolies. Look up and you will see a sign saying **Gadodia Market**. This is the entrance to Delhi's wholesale spice market. Turn into the darkened arcade and your olfactory response will be to sneeze and sneeze and sneeze again! The air here is thick with chilli, turmeric and asafoetida.

This market is about seventy years old and it is the largest spice market in Asia. If you want to buy fifty kilos of turmeric then this is the place to come. If you wish to purchase a more moderate amount you must buy it from one of the merchants out on the street as it is strictly wholesale here. Once you push your way through the darkened entrance you will come into a courtyard piled high with hessian bags. There are small offices all around the courtyard. This is where all the trading and weighing of the spices is conducted. Once that is done, it is all shipped back out on the backs of coolies or on the carts that you had to dodge to get in here.

Come out of the spice market and continue to your left. The street you are on is called Khari Baoli and the spice stalls give way to stalls selling *pickles and chutneys* (chutneys are sweet and often quite hot and pickles are hot and sour). The pickles and chutneys are displayed on saucers for prospective customers to visually inspect. Amongst these pickle shops there is a narrow lane on your left. This is **Gali Batasha** (Sugar Meringue Lane). This long laneway is populated with sugar merchants. You will see different types and grades of sugar displayed on large flat stainless-steel trays. In keeping with the sweet theme there are also merchants selling *candied fruit, sweet biscuits* and *packaged sweets*. You can also buy *varak*.

Depending on your energy levels you could continue up Khari Baoli to Sadar Bazaar. This is the wholesale market for stainless steel tableware. Be warned though that this is an endurance test as this part of Old Delhi is impossibly gridlocked with people, carts and rickshaws. If you don't fancy tackling the journey to Sadar Bazaar, you can buy the same tableware in stores throughout Delhi.

If you are visiting Old Delhi during Ramadan you may like to prolong your visit until dusk. Once the sun goes down, the area around the Jama Masjid comes alive as the hungry faithful head to food stalls and restaurants to break their daylight fast. If you haven't visited Karim's yet you might like to end your Mughal day with dinner there.

Four

∎

BRITISH DELHI

It was the lure of spices that first brought the British to India in the early seventeenth century. Spices had been a valuable and important commodity in Europe since medieval times but the spice trade between Europe and India had been dominated by the Dutch and the Portuguese. Looking to gain some control over the spice market and extract a greater profit for themselves, the British made their way to India. Although their initial intention had been simply to establish trading posts, they soon realized the enormous commercial potential of the land and their ambitions changed—the domination and control of India became their goal.

The British were not the only Europeans interested in India. The French had also begun to stake out Indian territory. This further aroused the British desire to control India. France and Britain had a long history of competing for territory and there was great animosity between the two countries. The British were determined to win India if only to prevent the French from doing so.

In 1756, the Seven Years' War broke out in Europe between the British and the French. By the time they emerged victorious from this prolonged battle in 1763, the British had quelled French ambition both in India and in Europe. Freed from the distraction of subduing their main rival, the British could now clearly focus on winning complete control of India.

In the hundred years between their arrival in India and in finally ousting the French, the British had not been idle in commercial matters. They were still another hundred years away from claiming India as British territory, but British business in India was well established. They had obtained many trade concessions from various Indian rulers and were always calculating to gain more. If diplomacy was unable to win them these concessions then violence often did. Regarding themselves as morally and culturally superior to the Indians, the British had no trouble justifying their subsequent colonization of the subcontinent.

The British had come to India in ships and they were reliant on ships to transport the goods of India back to Europe. Establishing trading ports was therefore integral to their success and they built port cities out of the coastal swamplands in Calcutta and Bombay. They also gained control of the important trading port of Madras from its native rulers. With their focus trained on India's coastline, the landlocked city of Delhi held little strategic appeal for the British. The early British envoys who visited Delhi had been sent there on diplomatic missions to gain trading dispensations. Several of these envoys spent long periods there trying to win the Emperor's favour, but they often failed to do so. The British lacked an understanding of the culture and style of conducting business in the Mughal court. Expecting straightforward interactions they were often bewildered and frustrated by the intricate machinations of conducting business in an oriental city with an imperious ruler. The prospect of gaining a foothold in Delhi seemed unlikely for the time being.

When the Mughal Emperor Aurangzeb died in 1707, the century following his death was one of great instability in Delhi. There were twelve Emperors crowned in this period, some reigning only for a few months. The longest rule, that of Muhammad Shah, lasted for twenty-nine years but was marred by the massacre and plunder of Delhi by the Afghan Nadir Shah in 1739. Twenty years later, a violent earthquake rocked the city shaking its political stability further. In 1803, assisted by French mercenaries, the Marathas (a central Indian tribe with Rajput ancestry) captured Delhi. They held the royal family captive in the palace and proceeded to torture them and threaten their lives. When the British General, Lord Lake, defeated the Marathas in Delhi later in that same year, the terrified and demoralized royal family welcomed their liberators with open arms.

These events not only gave the British a foothold in Delhi, it enabled them to take covert control of the city. They allowed the Emperor to remain on his throne but his power had been usurped. He was left with exclusive jurisdiction within the confines of the imperial palace but his powers stopped there. The laws outside the palace were administered in his name but he had no say in their development. He was no longer the Emperor of Hindustan but the 'King of Delhi'. The real power in Delhi now lay with the Resident (British government agent); the Emperor had become a mere figurehead.

Having gained control of Delhi the British began to reside in the city. The first British residents of Delhi initially sought to integrate themselves into the life of the city. Befitting their role as rulers they enthusiastically enjoyed a lifestyle that emulated that of Delhi's nobility. In the evenings they lounged in Indian-style pyjamas, smoking hookahs and chewing paan while watching Indian dancing girls. These men relished the local food and their evening's entertainment was always preceded by a feast of Mughal-style dishes. There were no women amongst Delhi's first British inhabitants, so the men kept harems of Indian wives. Delhi's first Resident, Sir David Ochterlony, promenaded himself and his Indian wives through the city every evening on elephants. This was a lifestyle that few British could ever have hoped to aspire to back in Britain.

However, the British were in Delhi (and India) for

economic gain and to facilitate this they quickly transformed Delhi from an imperial city into a commercial one. Delhi enjoyed a period of great prosperity between 1803 and 1857 as the British went about the task of 'civilizing' Delhi. To turn the city into an entrepôt of enterprise they completed extensive civil engineering works, built a new drainage system, cleaned and reopened canals and made attempts to improve sanitation. As they began to shape Delhi into their European idea of a city, they returned to the familiar habits of their British way of life. Wives and families had also begun to arrive and that dampened any further dalliances with local culture. 'Going native' had been but a pleasant interlude.

Quick to anticipate the desires of their new leading citizens, many of Delhi's merchants eased up on selling the jewellery and fine silks so profitable during the Mughal era and began to concentrate on stocking the merchandise that the British residents would pay well for. They did a brisk trade in imported tinned foods and wines and it didn't take long before Chandni Chowk was full of European comestibles. Merchants grew rich on the profits of imported food and drink. The British found the local food so inexpensive that they felt justified in paying exorbitant amounts for their shipped luxuries. These items were also some compensation to the British for the 'discomforts' of Indian life.

In 1857 the Indians revolted against the British. There

were outbreaks of fighting all over India but Delhi was the scene of some particularly brutal conflict. For two months the rebellious Indians besieged Delhi's British residents. Many of them were killed but the British eventually emerged the victors. Their success in Delhi was matched by Indian capitulation throughout the country and this gave the British the opening to finally claim India as their own. As punishment for his purported role in the 1857 Mutiny, the British exiled the last Mughal Emperor, Bahadur Shah, to Burma and publicly executed his heirs. As a further act of retaliation, the British banished Muslims from Delhi. Complete control of the city was now firmly in British hands; there was no longer the need to make a pretence of accommodating a Muslim monarch.

Delhi was a demoralized place post Mutiny but the British community there vigorously renewed their commercial activities and turned the city into the commercial capital of the Punjab and the Northern Provinces. After the Mutiny the control of India had passed out of the hands of the commercial East India Company and into that of the British government. This change did not diminish British enthusiasm for profitable enterprise. Delhi prospered and there was a flurry of civic building activity: the Town Hall, a grand railway station, a public library. There was also a concurrent boom in private building.

The events of the Mutiny had confirmed for the

British their opinion that Indians were not to be trusted. The British felt insecure and threatened inside the walls of Delhi; so they built their own enclave, **Civil Lines**, to the north of the city adjacent to the ridge. This was a curiosity to Delhi's native population as they could not understand why anybody would want to live outside the walls of the city. Amongst the spacious bungalows of Civil Lines several hotels that catered exclusively for Delhi's European citizens and their guests were built. Hotels **Cecil**, **Swiss** and **Maidens** were well patronized by memsahibs meeting for light refreshments and gossip during the day. In the evening these women would return with their sahibs for drinks, dinner and dancing. The hotels were also the venues for the British community's gala events. The Maidens Hotel boasted a commodious ballroom (capacity 2,000 people) that was the scene of a spectacular ball held to honour the visit of the Prince of Wales to Delhi in 1927.

The Cecil and the Swiss hotels no longer exist in Civil Lines; one is now a block of flats, the other altered beyond recognition. Maidens Hotel is the only survivor. Now owned by the Oberoi Group, the hotel has altered little since its heyday. The hotel's wide verandahs, where listless memsahibs once whiled away their time in its cool recesses sipping iced drinks, have been enclosed to accommodate the requirements of modern air conditioning, but this is the only change that has been made to its colonial form. The atmosphere of the Raj is captured here and the **Curzon**

Room is one of the few places in Delhi where you can enjoy a taste of British Delhi. In amongst the items of an Indian menu, you will find *mulligatawny soup* and *Dak Bungalow chicken*—a country-style roast chicken so called because it was the inevitable meal served in the dak bungalows the British built throughout northern India to accommodate themselves when required to travel. If you don't want to travel to the Maidens Hotel, this is an easy dish to make at home (traditionally made with a scrawny chicken, the dish benefits immeasurably from being made with a nice, plump hen).

■ *Roast Chicken Dak Bungalow Style* ■
Serves 4

Ingredients
1 cup curd
3 cloves garlic
2 tbsp freshly ground ginger
2 tbsp lemon juice
2 tsp freshly ground coriander seeds
$1/2$ tsp Kashmiri mirch (or cayenne pepper)
$1/2$ tsp turmeric
2 cups hot water
salt and freshly ground black pepper to taste
1 whole chicken (about 2 kg with or without skin)

Method
Combine all ingredients except chicken in a bowl. Mix well. Place chicken in bowl and cover with the mariande. Refrigerate for at least 4 hours or overnight.

Take chicken from the bowl and allow excess mariande to drain off.

Preheat oven to 180°C. Place chicken on a rack that fits inside an oven tray. Pour hot water into tray.

Cook chicken for 25 minutes on one side. Turn and cook for 25 minutes on the other. Increase heat to 200°C and cook chicken for a further 20-30 minutes. To check if chicken is cooked, poke a skewer between the leg and body. If the juice runs clear, chicken is done.

If coating on chicken starts to burn, cover chicken with foil for remaining baking time.

Other vestiges of the Raj you might like to enjoy at the Maidens are a *chhota peg* (small measure) of whisky made long with soda water and ice; a *gimlet* (gin and lime) or *gin and tonic* at the **Cavalry Bar**, or a pot of English-style *tea served with biscuits* in the manicured hotel gardens.

The British residing in Delhi were either in the employ of the government or they were boxwallahs (merchants and traders). They developed Delhi predominantly as a trading centre and were little concerned with developing industry there. The industries that did develop were often to manufacture items that the British felt were essential to a civilized life. One thing the British couldn't do without was biscuits and to satisfy a demand for these, the Hindu Biscuit Company began the manufacture of biscuits in Delhi in 1890. The factory had been set up with the aim of supplying the British community with biscuits but the biscuits caught on within the wider population. The company eventually became the aptly named Britannia Biscuit Company and you will see that name on advertising hoardings all over Delhi. Britannia biscuits are ubiquitous at tea stalls around the city, on the shelves of stores and in most Indian homes.

The majority of India's British inhabitants did not overly enjoy living in India. They were there to make money and to create an empire. They were so assured in their cultural superiority that India offered little interest to them and most of them found it a disquieting and threatening place (there were of course exceptions to this). The climate couldn't have been more different to that of England and the heat caused them extreme discomfort and illness. It was worse for the women who often had no choice but to accompany their husbands to India. They were bound by the social mores of the time to wear corsets, stockings, hats and layers of heavy undergarments, regardless of the weather. The accepted—and expected— British response to life in India was to ignore its differences and discomforts and to continue with life as if one was still living in England. The way the British lived in Bombay was little different to how they lived in Calcutta; their lifestyle was uniform throughout the country and this was no more evident than at their tables.

The British inhabitants of Delhi were no different in adherering to this formulaic pattern of living. Describing the culinary life of a British family resident in Delhi could be the description of the eating habits of any British family in India.

Breakfast

The day would start with *chhota hazari* (little breakfast), *tea* and perhaps a *piece of fruit*. This was followed by a rigorous horse ride up along the ridge or out the southern gate of the city around the crumbling monuments of older cities. If riding was not undertaken, then some social work or social calling would occur. Breakfast was at ten and it inevitably consisted of *rice*, *fish*, *eggs*, *preserves* and *tea* or *coffee*. Other popular breakfast items were *devilled meats* (leftover meat spruced up with spices), *fish stew*, *fresh fruit*, *pie*, *beer* and *iced claret* in summer. As there was no refrigeration, fish was always eaten at breakfast for fear of it putrefying if kept throughout the day. In Delhi, the fish was caught in the Yamuna and a servant was dispatched early morning to purchase it.

Kedgeree was a popular dish on British breakfast tables in India. Incorporating fish and rice it owes its name and concept to the Indian dish of lentils and rice, called khichdi.

■ *Kedgeree* ■
Serves 4

Ingredients
4 tbsp butter
2 tbsp chopped onion
a pinch of nutmeg

$^1/_2$ tsp ground cinnamon
$^1/_2$ tsp ground allspice (kabab chini)
3 cups (500 g) long grain rice
$1^1/_2$ (125 g) dal (soaked in water for 1 hour)
salt to taste
250 g cooked smoked fish
2 hard boiled eggs
freshly chopped parsley for garnish

Method

Melt butter in a pan, add onion and spices and cook until onion is soft but not brown. Add rice and drained dal and cook for a few minutes. Add salt and enough boiling water to cover mixture, cover pan and cook until rice and dal are ready (about 30 minutes), adding more boiling water if necessary. Leave the rice mixture to steam for 5-10 minutes. Serve on a platter with fish flaked over the top along with sliced hard boiled eggs, a good sprinkling of parsley and a grinding of black pepper.

'Devilled' dishes were to be found both on the breakfast and the lunch table but they were most welcome for breakfast as they were considered to aid a rapid recovery from a hangover—and as hangovers were a very regular occurrence for some, this was important (see section on drinking further on in the chapter).

■ *Devilled Eggs* ■
Serves 3-4

Ingredients
6 hard-boiled eggs
1 tsp mustard powder

salt to taste
freshly ground black pepper to taste
$^1/_2$ tsp cayenne pepper
4 tbsp mayonnaise
1 tbsp Worcestershire sauce
1 tsp curry powder
finely chopped parsley for garnish

Method

Cut boiled eggs in half lengthwise. Remove yolks.

Mix yolks with all other ingredients except curry powder and parsley. Blend until smooth.

Refill egg whites with yolk mixture by either piling it back in with a spoon or piping it in with a piping bag and wide nozzle.

Sprinkle with curry powder and parsley.

Lunch

Lunch was at noon and a typical lunch would include *European-style soup*, *roast meat*, *pie*, *cheese*, *dessert* and wine. An adjective commonly used to describe these lunch tables was 'groaning'. Early on in their stay, British residents would have engaged in a round of social engagements after lunch but no matter how determined they were to ignore the fact that they lived in a foreign land, they could not always ignore the climate and soon had to make some concessions to it. Afternoon social rounds gave way to afternoon siestas and social calls were made in the morning with guests often being invited for breakfast. It was not done to invite guests to lunch and only close family members ate this meal together (my theory on this is that the searing midday heat left most people sweaty, cross, uncomfortable and not fit for company).

Dinner

Dinner was typically an elaborate affair and preferably taken in company. Throwing and attending dinner parties was the principal form of evening entertainment for the British in Delhi. Dinner was also the chance for the hostess to show off her culinary best and that usually meant imported tinned foods. Never before have *canned foods* enjoyed such high esteem: canned mushrooms, asparagus, pate, salmon, herrings, cheese and ham graced the tables accompanied by imported spirits and wines. There would also be a number of 'Anglo-Indian' dishes created under instructions from the memsahib by her native cook.

Anglo-Indian Cuisine

(I use the term 'Anglo-Indian' in its pre-1911 usage, for people of direct British descent living in India i.e. both parents British. After 1911 the term 'Anglo-Indian' was used to distinguish 'people of mixed parentage who had a European ancestor from their male line of inheritance'.)

The deployment of small armies of domestic servants was one aspect of Indian life that the British living in India willingly adopted. In the servant hierarchy, the household cook was at the top and he would have daily conferences with 'madam' regarding the family's culinary requirements. These meetings were very often a source of frustration to both parties for neither spoke the other's language. Although memsahib may have had the means and the time to study Hindi or Urdu, she very rarely had the inclination to do so preferring to leave it to her husband. It was inevitable then that the instructions that were given to the cook were misunderstood—both linguistically and culturally—and that familiar dishes would not appear in the anticipated form. Memsahib was also up against her cook's tendency to 'Indianize' food, which meant adding plenty of masala to everything. Many of these 'spiced up' versions of European dishes were not appealing to the British palate but some were and these were duly noted. These then became the recipes that were passed from one memsahib to another, eventually finding their way into the cookbooks that became the culinary prescriptions by which the memsahib set her table.

These popular cookbooks were also full of recipes for Indian dishes that had been anglicized. The broader contacts that the sahib had with Indian culture meant that he often developed a taste for spiced food and in order to please her mate, memsahib would allow 'milder' versions of Indian dishes onto her table. The British also had to acknowledge that the well-spiced cooking of Indians was efficacious in the hot weather, the spices being of great benefit to digestion and to cooling of the body. Perhaps the best-known and one of the most successful creations of this often awkward culinary marriage is the mulligatawny soup that became an inevitable inclusion on the tables of British India. This soup evolved from the simple *rasam* of South India that is served over rice.

■ *Mulligatawny Soup* ■
Serves 8-10

Ingredients

2 cloves garlic, crushed
3-cm piece ginger, finely chopped
1 tsp cayenne pepper
1 tsp turmeric powder
1 tsp coriander powder
1 tsp cumin powder
1 bay leaf
1 tbsp vegetable oil
2 tbsp ghee
I large onion, finely chopped
the meat from 4 boned and skinned chicken thighs, diced
(reserve bones)
$^3/_4$ cup coconut milk
$1^1/_2$ litres chicken stock
6 tbsp dal (toor, arhar or masoor dal)
1 tsp tamarind concentrate or 2 tbsp tamarind pulp
dissolved in 4 tbsp boiling water, strained
3 tbsp rice
$^1/_2$ tsp crushed roasted cumin and coriander seeds
fresh coriander leaves finely chopped for garnish

Method

Place first 8 ingredients in a food processor or grinder and process into a paste.

Heat ghee in a large saucepan and fry onion, stirring over moderate heat until golden. Add spice purée from processor and continue to fry and stir for 3 minutes, until spices are well cooked and mellowed.

Add chicken meat and bones and stir for 1 more minute. Pour in coconut milk and let mixture simmer, uncovered for 5 minutes.

Pour in chicken stock and add dal; stir and cover pan. Bring barely to a boil, reduce heat and let soup simmer for 30 minutes, or until the dal has totally disintegrated and onion is soft enough to squash against the side of the pan. Cook for 15 minutes till dal is half done, add rice and cook another 15 minutes.

Strain out meat and rice on to a plate and discard bones. Purée soup in batches in a blender and then return it to the pan over heat. Stir in tamarind until dissolved, bring soup just to the point of boiling again.

Turn off heat and pour soup into a tureen or into individual soup bowls. Add cooked meat and rice. Sprinkle with cumin/coriander mixture and garnish with coriander leaves.

After mulligatawny, *Country Captain* was the Anglo-Indian dish which would have appeared most regularly on the tables of Delhi's British residents. **Yellow Brick Road** offers both mulligatawny and Country Captain on its menu along with some other Anglo-Indian-inspired dishes. Yellow Brick Road is one of Delhi's perennially fashionable cafes (it was recently voted one of Delhi's top five eating places even though those who voted admitted that it was predominantly the place itself and not the food that won their vote). There is also a small selection of Anglo-Indian dishes on the menu at the currently *tres* fashionable **Daniell's Tavern**. If these 'hot' spots are putting Anglo-Indian dishes on their menus it must mean that this style of cuisine is making a comeback. This recipe for Country Captain will put you ahead of the fashion pack.

■ *Country Captain* ■
Serves 4-6

Ingredients
1/2 cup ghee
1 kg chicken pieces
4 large onions, finely sliced
3 cloves garlic, crushed
1 tsp turmeric powder
1 tbsp finely chopped or grated fresh ginger
3 green chillies, seeded and finely chopped
1 cup hot chicken stock
salt to taste
2 tbsp lime juice
1 tsp freshly ground black pepper

Method
Heat ghee in pan over medium heat. Fry chicken pieces until browned on all sides. Remove from ghee.

Fry a generous handful of the onions in the ghee until crisp and golden. Remove and drain on kitchen paper.

Add remaining onions, garlic and ginger to the ghee. Sauté until softened.

Add turmeric, chillies and salt. Stir well. Add chicken pieces and stir to coat with the onion/spice mix.

Add chicken stock, cover pan, turn heat to low and simmer

for 20 minutes or until chicken is tender. Just before the cooking is finished add lime juice and black pepper. (This dish should be quite dry with little or no liquid remaining in the pan.)

Serve hot garnished with the crisp fried onions.

Servants

One of the chief topics of conversation amongst the British in India concerned the habits of their domestic servants and it was the habits of the cook that came in for the most discussion. It was a constant source of frustration to the memsahib that the cook would not do things her way. The British installed waist-high benches in their kitchens for chopping and preparation and could not understand why the cook and his accomplices ignored these and continued to work in their customary way, squatting over low stools.

Memsahib spent much of her time being concerned with hygiene and was usually convinced that her cook was doing something filthy in the kitchen. The British grapevine was plump with urban myths about cooks— that they stirred the rice pudding with their fingers or that they strained the custard/sauce/stock through sahib's dirty socks or their own soiled turban. The smart memsahib soon understood that her life would be easier if she turned a blind eye to the habits of her cook. Others spent their entire stay in India pointlessly trying to 'train' their cooks. No matter how much of a frenzy memsahib worked herself into over her cook's habits, he was not going to change.

He could rarely see the sense in what he was being asked to do. The memsahib's insistence on roasting and baking in such a hot climate must have appeared ludicrous to him. It would never have occurred to these overconfident British that their Indian servants may have found their habits filthy. The British kept their toilets inside the house and their kitchens outside, a practice that was considered foul to Indian sensibilities. The Emperor Shah Jahan once commented that the British had two major faults: eating pork and not washing themselves after they had excreted bodily wastes.

Tiffin

As the restraint and moral rigour of the Victorian era gave way to the liveliness and comparative frivolity of the Edwardian period, the British in India loosened their stays. The British may have considered that they had gone someway towards civilizing India but they could do nothing to control the heat. As much as they had tried to live as if they were at home in Bath or Scarborough, the weather eventually got the better of them and the pattern of their lives had to be readjusted to accommodate India's climate.

There was also the dawning realization that the consumption of large amounts of heavy food was injurious to health in such heat. The midday meal of their forefathers moved its time slot to 2.00 p.m. and the groaning table of

soups, roast meats, puddings and cheeses gave way to a
lighter lunch usually referred to as 'tiffin'. An Anglo-Indian
'curry' was typically included for tiffin ('curry' is an Anglo-
Indian invention and it is not a dish that Indians would
recognize by that name as such. Taken from the Tamil
word for sauce, *karhi*, the British turned it into the generic
term now used to describe any wet, spicy dish).

If a curry was not served at tiffin, meat from the
previous night's dinner often returned to the table. There
were several different guises under which it could reappear:
devilled, as *meat balls*, *shepherd's pie* or as *chops* or *cutlets*. A
distinctly Anglo-Indian way to use up leftover meat was
jhal fry or *jhalfrezie*.

■ *Jhal Fry* ■
Serves 4

Ingredients
a walnut-size piece of tamarind
2 tbsp ghee
2 large onions, sliced
1 tsp cumin powder
1 tsp turmeric powder (or substitute 2 tsp curry powder
for the cumin and turmeric)
2 fresh green chillies, sliced
500 g leftover beef or lamb
1 tsp salt

Method
Soak tamarind in $1/2$ cup of boiling water for 5 minutes.
Push tamarind through a sieve with the back of a spoon (you

will be left with the seeds and some skin in the sieve, discard).

Heat ghee in a pan and fry onions until crisp and golden.

Add spices, chillies, meat, salt and tamarind paste and cook until sauce is a rich brown and liquid has reduced.

Serve with rice and mango chutney.

The heavy steamed and baked puddings that the British were so fond of gave way at tiffin to *jellies*, *whipped fruit creams*, *stewed fruit* and even *ice-cream* when amenities allowed for its preparation. Indian cooks also developed a reputation for making good *soufflés* and these were served at both lunch and dinner.

■ *Mango and Ginger Soufflé* ■
Serves 6

Ingredients
2 mangoes, peeled and chopped (or 1 cup
canned mango pulp)
2 tsp powdered ginger
1 litre water
a little extra butter and sugar for the soufflé dish
1 cup cream
1 cup water
2 tbsp plain white flour
1 cup castor sugar
pinch of salt
2 tbsp unsalted butter
6 eggs, separated

Method
Cook mango and ginger in 1 litre water until mango is soft and water is absorbed.

Butter a large soufflé dish or 6 individual dishes, sprinkle with a little sugar and shake out the excess.

Mix cream, 1 cup water, flour, $3/4$ cup of the sugar and a pinch of salt into the top of a double boiler. Whisk over the heat until the mixture is smooth and slightly thickened. Add the butter and whisk through the mixture until it is smooth and shiny.

Remove pan from heat and add mango mixture. Set aside.

Beat egg yolks until pale and creamy and add to mango mixture. Return pan to the heat in the top of the double boiler and cook until mixture thickens.

Whip egg whites until they form soft peaks. Add remaining sugar and beat until egg whites are glossy. Fold $1/3$ of the egg whites into mango mix with a spatula or metal spoon to lighten mixture. Gently fold in remaining egg whites.

Pour into soufflé dish and bake at 190°C for 45 minutes. Serve hot. If using individual dishes, reduce cooking time to 35 minutes.

The new lunch hour pushed dinner to a much later time slot, but the formality of dinner was never challenged. Indian-style dishes now only ever appeared on the British table at lunchtime. By the beginning of the twentieth century, the evening meal had become the preserve of French-style cooking that was the vogue in Delhi. One can only imagine the dishes that must have appeared. Memsahib may have loosened her corsets at the dawn of the new century, but she was still up against the same difficulties in her kitchen. She still had an Indian cook who cooked on a charcoal stove, with whom she shared no language with which to explain the nuances of French cooking—that is if she understood them herself. The menus may have read *pate foie gras, bouillabaisse, pigeons truffé a la Perigord, cochon de lait, petits bouchers aux huitres* and *gateau St. Honore* but what appeared on the table would have, in all likelihood, borne only passing resemblance to its namesake (imagine the difficulty of producing fine French patisserie in such a hot, humid climate in an era when refrigeration was rudimentary and air conditioning did not exist).

Drinking

The British in India were renowned for their heavy consumption of alcohol. Some made claims that it helped to restore an appetite in hot weather, others that it was efficacious in the prevention of malaria and fever. For some it was merely a way to pass the time or to allay loneliness and alienation. Social rules about alcohol consumption were strict though and it was not often that any Britisher overstepped them. Alcoholic drinks were not taken before 6.00 p.m.—with an exception made for weekends. It was also not done to appear 'drunk' though it was perfectly acceptable to consume large quantities of alcohol—as long as you could keep the effects under wraps!

When the British first came to India, they had had to be satisfied with local liquors such as *arrack*. To make them more palatable they drank these native brews mixed with sugar, spices, water and lime juice—the original *punch*. ('Punch' originated from the Hindi word for five, 'panch'.) As they settled into India, the British began to import the drinks they were familiar with—*brandy*, *gin*, *whisky*, *beer* and *wine*. They then imported the equipment and the expertise with which to produce these liquors themselves (with the exception of wine which continued to come from Persia or Europe). They also produced *rum* which was a by-product of the flourishing Indian sugar industry.

Once they had secured supply of their favourite liquors, the British needed something with which to mix and extend their drinks. This spurred the beginning of the carbonated beverage industry in India. *Soda water* and *tonic water* were the most popular carbonated drinks amongst the British. Tonic water contained quinine as a preventative against the malaria that had taken such a heavy toll on British lives in India. Soda water was an aid to digestion in the hot weather and was recommended by doctors as a general tonic. *Whisky with soda* and *gin and tonic* were the quintessential drinks of British India.

An essential component of any of these drinks was plenty of ice and the British were also responsible for the development of *mechanized ice manufacture* in Delhi.

The most significant drinking habit that the British introduced to Delhi, though, was that of *drinking tea*. The Mughal Emperors had enjoyed tea and the British had been tea drinkers before they reached India, but all this tea had come from China. When the British discovered Assamese tribals drinking native wild tea in the 'Indian Highlands', they saw in it commercial potential. Despite a shaky start, they persevered until they had built a successful tea-growing industry in India.

Tea is no longer the exclusive drink of the aristocracy; it is now a common and inexpensive drink in Delhi and throughout India. The Indians have developed their own style of drinking tea. *Desi chai* is made by stewing the tea in milk with plenty of sugar and pungent spices such as cardamom and cloves. This will usually be the only style of tea available at small tea stalls in Delhi but most hotels and restaurants should be able to furnish you with 'tray tea' (tea in a pot with separate milk and sugar).

New Delhi

In 1911, Delhi was proclaimed the new capital of India. The announcement came at a spectacular durbar held in Delhi to honour the presence of the Emperor and Empress of India, George V and Queen Mary (millions of rupees were spent on this durbar while famine raged in the districts surrounding Delhi). The motions for building this new city were underway almost immediately—George V laid the foundation stone of New Delhi three days after the announcement. While the construction of New Delhi was underway, the Viceroy of India (the Viceroy ruled on behalf of a sovereign) and his associated retinue took up temporary quarters in Civil Lines. This was a period of great expansion and activity for Delhi's British community and Civil Lines was awash with parties and celebratory balls. French champagne flowed profusely as they confidently built the new capital of the empire they expected to rule forever.

After nearly three decades of building, New Delhi was officially declared open in 1930. It quickly became the focus of British life in Delhi, and indeed India, for all the official business of administrating the country now happened there. New Delhi's spacious boulevards were lined with the bungalow homes of those employed in official endeavour and the new commercial area of Connaught Circus (Place) was full of stores selling the best of imported European goods. There were also a number of restaurants that thrived there, serving *continental cuisine* and acting as meeting places for New Delhi's British residents, politicians, journalists and well-heeled. **United Coffee House** and **Standard Restaurant** are two stalwarts from this era that are still going strong. United Coffee House has an immaculately preserved 1940s interior and it is well-patronized by locals and tourists. All day the doors swing open and shut with people coming in for a full-scale meal, a snack or just to sit and watch the passing trade over a coffee or a beer. The United maintains a genteel air but gone are the days when restaurants in Connaught Place were the exclusive preserve of Delhi's upper crust.

The clientele is a much more diverse mix of people these days and the extensive menus aims to please all patrons. Standard Restaurant hasn't been preserved quite as well as United Coffee House but it has remained well-patronized for more than half a century. The main attraction here is the huge light-filled space overlooking the Connaught Place gardens. Tucked up here in front of the floor-to-ceiling windows with a *chilled beer* (the British introduced beer brewing in India), you can enjoy watching the non-stop daily activity of New Delhi's modern inhabitants as it unfolds in front of you.

The crowning glory of New Delhi was Viceroy House (now Rashtrapati Bhavan), the residence of the Viceroy of India. This enormous palace had been fitted out to host regal parties and in its basements there was a full-scale bakery to produce *European-style breads* and *baked goods*. The Viceroy entertained there in grand style and it was the most prestigious social honour to be invited to a dinner, a ball or garden party at the Viceregal residence.

While the stolidness of the Victorian era had been shed, the social rules that governed daily British life in India had really altered very little by the 1930s. The rigmaroles of official protocol were still considered indispensable. Food was considered somewhat dispensable, though, and although the structure of official social functions did not change, the content did. Guests no longer had to sit through the rigours of the meat-dominated multi-coursed dinners so favoured by earlier British rulers of the empire. Meals were lighter and the courses fewer and this change not only eased the burden on the guests' digestion but on the Viceroys' budget as well. As an austerity measure during the Second World War, the then Viceroy, Lord Mountbatten, served *spam and potato* at Viceregal dinners. When Congress leaders were invited to dine at Viceregal House, the Mountbattens ensured that the menu was exclusively *vegetarian* out of deference to their wishes.

New Delhi would not have been complete without a grand hotel and in between invitations to the Viceroy's palace, Delhi's British community acquitted themselves very well in the elegant dining rooms, colonnaded arcades and tranquil gardens of the newly built **Hotel Imperial**. The hotel's glamorous opening dinner hosted by the Vicereine, Lady Willingdon, was the social highlight of 1935. While now a decidedly modern hotel in its amenities, the appearance of the Imperial remains largely unchanged since 1935 and subsequent renovations have enhanced its historic character. There is still a strong whiff of the colonial in the ambience here. The marble hallways entice you with the promise of encountering some ghostly human remnant of the Raj but short of that, you can just enjoy another chhota peg or some chilled local beer in the intimate atmosphere of the **Patiala Peg**. The prints and photographs of the Patiala regiment that tastefully crowd the walls should satisfy those with a passion for Indian

military history. For those with less armorial interest, tea
on the lawn beneath the swaying palm trees is a pleasure
that those British living in New Delhi circa 1935 would
have also enjoyed.

Picnics

When not enjoying the outdoors on the lawns of exclusive
hotels, the British community were often to be found
picnicking amongst the crumbling ruins of Delhi's earlier
inhabitants. To satisfy appetites stimulated by explorations
around the decaying monuments or by some inspired
flirting in the romantically charged atmosphere, these
picnics were always well-catered-for affairs. Aided by a
retinue of servants, guests were served *cold meats—canned
ham, turkey* and *beef* if they could get it—with an array of
*condiments, game pies, pressed tongue, rissoles, sandwiches,
cheese, biscuits, cake,* and *chocolates.* Indian foods such as
aloo parantha, shami kababs and *nargisi kofta* (similar to
Scotch eggs) were also included. All this largesse would be
accompanied by *nimbu pani, chilled beer* and *champagne.*
To finish up, the servants would build a small fire and *tea
and coffee* would be served.

The once sparsely populated plains that surrounded
New Delhi are now filled with the roads, homes and
businesses of a bustling modern city but you can still visit
the same ruins that were the venues for such elaborate
picnics. To put yourself in the shoes of the departed British,

you could take a picnic to Lodi Gardens, Humayun's Tomb, Siri Fort gardens, or the municipal park behind the Qutab Minar. If you are a bit short on servants to stage the sort of affair described above, then head to **Wengers** in Connaught Place. Here you will be able to put together an admirable picnic from their range of European-style sandwiches, savouries, cakes and dainties. Wengers packs their goods in boxes which makes them perfect for transporting to picnic sites. Or make up these picnic goodies yourself.

■ *Nargisi Kofta* ■
Makes 10 pieces

Ingredients
1 tbsp ghee
3 medium onions, finely chopped
1 clove garlic, crushed
1 kg finely minced lamb or mutton
2 tsp salt
$1/3$ cup gram flour (besan)
10 hard boiled eggs, shelled
1 tsp garam masala powder (see chapter 'Mughal Delhi'
for recipe)
2 eggs, lightly beaten
$1/2$ tsp cumin powder
$1/2$ tsp cayenne powder
2 tsp coriander powder
ghee or oil for deep frying

Method
Heat 1 tbsp ghee over medium heat and gently cook onions and garlic until softened.

Place all ingredients except boiled eggs into a food processor and process into a smooth paste.

Divide mixture into 10 parts. Shape each into a patty 10 cm in diameter.

Dip each hard boiled egg in water and place in the centre of a patty. Work meat around egg until it is entirely enclosed by the meat. Smooth over any cracks.

Heat oil in a kadhai, wok or large pan and deep fry kofta until golden. Drain on kitchen paper.

■ *Dilli Picnic Sandwiches* ■
Makes 6 pieces

Ingredients
$^1/_2$ cup canned tuna
$^1/_2$ cup canned sardines, bones removed
1 tbsp mango chutney
2 hard-boiled egg yolks
1 tsp curry powder
2 tbsp finely chopped parsley
2 tbsp mayonnaise
freshly ground black pepper to taste
12 slices bread (white or brown)
butter to spread on bread slices

Method
Blend all ingredients except bread and butter using either a food processor or mortar and pestle, or mash together with a fork.

Spread the bread with a thin film of butter. Divide the filling evenly across 6 slices and spread.

Top with the remaining slices.

Remove crusts and cut into fingers or triangles.

Serve immediately or wrap in a damp cloth and store in an airtight container all ready for your picnic.

British Culinary Impact

Unlike those of previous rulers, the culinary habits of the British in Delhi had little impact on the food of most of Delhi's citizens. The British had preferred to keep India at a distance and effectively walled themselves off from the Indian population. When they left, they took their food with them. The only 'locals' on whom their culinary habits had had any significant influence were Delhi's elite upper class. The majority of the city's population still ate the same food that they had been eating since long before the British arrived. New Delhi's skies remained cloudy from the smoke of thousands of cow-dung fires over which the common Hindu meal of *dal, roti* and *rice* was cooked. In Old Delhi the air was still thick with the perfumed air of *spiced kababs*. It is a great irony that after all their efforts to keep India at arms length, the British actually took the taste for Indian cuisine home with them while only fragments of their cuisine remain. (One in every three meals eaten outside the home or as takeaway in Britain is Indian. Chicken tikka, samosa and 'curry' are as common as fish and chips.)

Before the British arrived, Delhi had been a city unto itself with its own language (Urdu), culture and food. The pre-British inhabitants of Delhi had been happy to live enclosed within the city walls and most found little need to venture beyond these. Focussed only on their own ends and threatened by an alien culture, the British tore down the walls of Delhi, brought in the railway and made their new city the seat of government. These actions brought many 'foreigners' to the city—Bengalis and Punjabis amongst others—and permanently changed its character. The British had swung open the doors of Delhi and they were about to be opened wider still.

MAIDENS HOTEL
7 Sham Nath Marg
Delhi 110 054
Tele: 23975464
Noon-Midnight

CURZON ROOM
Lunch 1 p.m.-3 p.m.
Dinner 7.30 p.m.-11 p.m.

CAVALRY BAR
11.00 a.m.-Midnight

YELLOW BRICK ROAD
Taj Ambassador Hotel
Sujan Singh Park
24632600
24 hours

DANIELL'S TAVERN
Hotel Imperial
Janpath
23341234, 23345678
12 p.m.-3 p.m. & 7.30 p.m.-11.30 p.m.

PATIALA PEG
Hotel Imperial
Janpath
23341234
11 a.m.-Midnight

UNITED COFFEE HOUSE
15-E Connaught Place
23322075, 23731697
9.30 a.m.-11.30 p.m.

STANDARD RESTAURANT
44 Regal Building
Connaught Place
23360048, 23365856
11 a.m.-11 p.m.

WENGERS
A-16 Connaught Place
23324373
10.30 a.m.-8 p.m.

■ Suggested tour

As suggested you might like to start your day with an al-fresco breakfast or brunch amidst the ruins that the British were so fond of riding around and picnicking at when they resided in Delhi. Visit Wengers in Connaught Place for some goodies to take with you and accompany these with some fruit from the **Oriental Fruit Store** (also in Connuaght Place) or from one of Delhi's many fruit vendors.

Lodi Gardens is the best place to go. The tombs in this park belong to the later Sultanate period and it was the British in the shape of Lady Willingdon who stepped in to save these medieval tombs from being destroyed during the development works of New Delhi. It was laid out as a park in the 1930s and prior to Partition, was called Lady Willingdon Gardens. Enjoy your breakfast on the lush green lawns and then take a stroll through the gardens. You might then like to explore British-built New Delhi. A good guide book will acquaint you with all the significant buildings. If you are in Delhi in late February or March, you must pay a visit to the Mughal Gardens at Rashtrapati Bhavan (despite the name, the Mughals did not lay out these gardens, the British did).

Once you have taken in the civic and administrative buildings of New Delhi, head over to the former British residential area of Civil Lines (you will need your own car or hire a car for this). Make your first stop at the Oberoi Maidens Hotel for lunch in the **Curzon Room**. The afternoon could then be spent visiting the Ridge and the Mutiny Memorial. There are still some of the bungalow-style homes that the British built in Civil Lines and you will notice the contrast between the wide open streets of this British-built suburb and the narrow, snaking lanes and alleyways of neighbouring Old Delhi. Not being accustomed to hot climates, the British did not understand the Indian system of building narrow lanes that blocked out the searing rays of the sun. The British took refuge from the heat in the shaded verandahs that they built surrounding their homes.

When you have finished in Civil Lines, head back across town to Connaught Place, the commercial hub of New Delhi, and to the Imperial Hotel. Take afternoon tea on the lawn under the palms or if the hour is right, you might like to enjoy a drink at the Patiala Peg. Try a gimlet or a whiskey-soda for refreshment Raj style.

∎

Five

DELHI AFTER PARTITION: a city of refugees

What we can eat and drink is ours. Whatever is left can go to
Ahmed Shah the invader.

—Punjabi saying

At midnight on 15 August 1947 the streets of Delhi were filled with cries of jubilation as the British cut India loose from the shackles of the Empire. Those who had not stayed up to cheer the precise moment of separation woke to find themselves citizens of an independent country and for many, it was an alien nation. The sounds of triumph soon gave way to cries of horror as the British drew an arbitrary line through their former dominion and partitioned her into India and Pakistan. This parting blow gave rise to one of the most tragic and bloody events of modern history.

Many Hindus who found themselves in Muslim Pakistan and many Muslims who remained in India were forced to flee to the other side. Many of them took nothing with them, grateful to escape with their lives intact. The confusion and fear created by the division of India into two separate nations engendered a level of violence so brutal that it remains chilling to speak of. Hindus butchered Muslims, Muslims slaughtered Hindus; trains crossing the newly created India-Pakistan border arrived at their destinations dripping blood to disgorge their cargo of slaughtered human beings. By partitioning India, the British created an ugly Muslim-Hindu divide in a country where the two groups had amicably coexisted for centuries.

The immediate effects of Partition were most keenly felt in the Punjab region which stretched from the banks of the Indus to the edges of Delhi. The new borders had sliced the Punjab in half and it became a tumultuous corridor through which its heterogeneous population of Muslims and Hindus tried to make their way to safety. The destination for many of these people was Delhi; scared and disorientated, the confines of the city represented a refuge to them. In a matter of weeks Delhi was a changed city.

Many of Delhi's Muslims had hurriedly fled to Pakistan in fear of their lives and their abandoned homes and businesses were taken over by newcomers who had arrived in the city after escaping the same fate elsewhere. As a result, Delhi received more people than she had unwillingly given up. Prior to Partition, Delhi had been a city of nearly one million people, predominantly Muslims; after Partition she became a city of close to two million people, an overwhelming majority of whom were Hindus. Delhi was quite literally bursting at the seams and this 'urban island in a rural sea' was forced to expand her boundaries.

The population of Delhi had been steadily growing ever since the city was crowned capital in 1911, but the influx of people after Partition was a virtual human explosion (there was a ninety per cent growth in population between 1940 and 1950). To accommodate her new inhabitants, Delhi expanded rapidly and a dozen or so hastily created colonies abutted the fringes of Old and New Delhi.

Punjab

The majority of refugees who settled in Delhi aftre Partition were Hindus and Sikhs from the Punjab. Optimistic people by nature, they gradually recovered from the shock, upheaval and loss that had beset them and began to take up the opportunities the city afforded. As they set about creating new lives for themselves, they also began to change the culinary life of the city.

Watered by five rivers—Beas, Chenab, Ravi, Sutlej and Jhelum—the Punjab is a marvellously fecund region and agriculture is the predominant industry. To the Punjabis, the ownership of fertile land on which to grow crops is the greatest wealth of all. Even urban Punjabis maintain direct contact with the land. The sound of the wind as it gently buffets a field of golden wheat and the vivid yellow of endless mustard fields are essential ingredients of life and cuisine for Punjabis. Indicative of its rural roots, typical Punjabi food is hearty, flavourful and substantial without artifice and fuss. *Wheat*, made into a variety of *flat breads*, *corn*, *mustard greens*, *dairy products* and *pulses* such as chana (chickpeas/gazbanos), *kali dal* (black lentils) and *rajma* (red kidney beans) are the staple foods of Punjab.

Often unable to take up their former occupations, many of the Punjabis who had ended up in Delhi began to eke out livelihoods by selling the food they were familiar with. With so many of their own in the city the demand for such food was strong. Lacking material resources, many started by setting up street stalls selling fried snacks such as *pakoras* (vegetable fritters) and inexpensive dishes such as *chana bhatura* (also called chholé bhaturé). What they lacked in resources the Punjabis made up with ingenuity and hard work and they turned many small food stalls into successful restaurants and catering businesses. Chana bhatura became the ubiquitous snack of Delhi, sold by hundreds of street vendors, in cafes and hotels and fast-food chains. Delhiites will all have their own favourite chana bhatura vendor and to single any one of them out as being the best is a difficult task (particularly when the location given is 'the guy on the side of the road as you turn left out of Amar Colony onto the Ring Road'). It could be safely said though, that the best chana bhatura is to be found on the streets.

■ *Chana/Chholé* ■
Serves 6

Ingredients

1¹/₂ cups dried chickpeas (Kabuli chana)
pinch of soda bicarbonate (optional)
1 tsp turmeric powder
2 black cardamoms
3-cm stick cinnamon
3 tbsp ghee or mustard oil
1 tsp cumin seeds
2 medium onions, sliced
2 tbsp crushed garlic
2 tbsp minced ginger
2 green chillies, seeded and finely chopped
salt to taste
2 bay leaves
1 tbsp garam masala powder
1 tsp coriander powder
1 tsp mango powder (amchur)
¹/₂ tsp red chilli powder (or to taste)
3 tomatoes, skinned and puréed
finely chopped fresh coriander leaves for garnish

Method

Soak chickpeas overnight with the bicarbonate.

Drain chickpeas, rinse and cook in 10 cups water over medium heat with turmeric, cardamom and cinnamon until chickpeas are tender but whole and water is absorbed (add more water if necessary). Discard whole spices.

While chickpeas are cooking, heat ghee or oil and fry cumin seeds until they sputter, add onion, garlic, ginger, green chillies, salt and bay leaves and cook until softened.

Add garam masala, coriander powder, mango powder and

chilli powder, and cook for a few minutes more. Add tomatoes and cook sauce over low heat for 10 minutes, stirring regularly.

Mix sauce through chickpeas (which should still be hot). Serve hot (preferably), warm or as a cold salad-type dish garnished with coriander leaves.

Sometimes this dish has potatoes in it. You can simply boil up 2-3 potatoes, skin and dice them and add them to the dish at the end.

■ *Bhatura* ■
Makes 10 pieces

Ingredients
3 tbsp curd
1 tbsp melted ghee
8 tbsp warm water
1 tsp sugar
1 cup plain flour (maida)
1 cup wholemeal flour (atta)
1 tsp soda bicarbonate
$^1/_2$ tsp salt
ghee or oil for frying

Method
Mix together curd, warm water and sugar.

Sift the flours, soda bicarbonate and salt together. Make a well in the centre and add curd mixture. Mix together to form a soft dough.

Place dough in a greased bowl and cover with a damp cloth. Place in a warm place and leave until dough swells to twice its size (4-5 hours).

Knead dough again and divide into 10 equal parts. Shape into balls and roll or pat out into rounds about 10 cms in diameter. Keep covered.

Heat oil or ghee in a kadhai, wok or large pan until hot, and deep fry the bhaturé, one at a time, until puffed up and golden. Drain briefly on kitchen paper and serve straight away with the chana.

Kanji is a typical Punjabi drink that you will find sold on Delhi streets. If you can source black carrots, it is very easy to make (it is not the same made with orange or red carrots).

■ *Kanji* ■
Makes about 4 litres

Ingredients
1 kg black carrots
2 tbsp black mustard seeds, ground
2 tbsp red chilli powder or to taste
2 tbsp salt
4 litres hot water

Method
Peel carrots and chop roughly.
Mix all ingredients together.
Put into a bottle or jar and seal tightly.
Place in the sun for 5-6 days. Shake the bottle regularly.
Strain liquid and serve chilled, garnished with fresh mint leaves and lime slices.

The number of Punjabis in Delhi and their growing economic success ensured that they began to dominate the food life of the city. Their preference for chicken over mutton soon saw Delhi become a city of poultry fanciers. It was the Punjabis who introduced Delhi to tomatoes. The *lachha* (slices of tomato, onion and lemon and whole green chillies) that accompanies most restaurant meals in Delhi is a Punjabi invention. The Punjabi's passion for dairy products, *paneer* in particular, saw a plethora of dishes based on combining this fresh soft cheese with favourite Punjabi foods: *matar paneer* (with peas), *paneer makhani* (with butter), *saag paneer* (with leafy greens), *paneer kali mirch* (with pepper). Modern Delhi restauranteurs are always looking for new paneer dishes with which to entice patrons. While there are always eager patrons wiling to try these new concoctions, it is the stalwart paneer dishes such as matar paneer, with which they anchor their menus, that people keep coming back for.

■ *Matar Paneer* ■
Serves 4

Ingredients
1 cup paneer (see recipe below)
2 tbsp ghee or butter
1 tsp cumin seeds
1 tbsp minced ginger
a tbsp crushed garlic
1 tsp garam masala powder
2 tsp freshly ground coriander powder
$^1/_2$ tsp turmeric powder
salt to taste
$^1/_2$ tsp mango powder (amchur)
2 tomatoes, chopped
$1^1/_2$ cups water or whey from paneer
1 cup fresh shelled peas (frozen if must be but fresh are best in this dish)
freshly ground black pepper

Method

Cut paneer into cubes. Heat ghee in a frying pan and fry paneer until golden on all sides. Remove from ghee with a slotted spoon and drain on kitchen paper.

Add cumin seeds to ghee and cook until they sputter. Add ginger and garlic and cook for a few minutes until softened. Add garam masala, coriander powder, turmeric, salt and mango powder. Stir well. Add tomatoes. Cook for 10 minutes.

Add water or whey and peas. Cook until peas are tender. Add paneer and black pepper. Serve hot.

■ Paneer ■

Ingredients
$3^{1}/_{4}$ cups milk
6 tbsp lime juice or white vinegar

Method

Bring milk to boil. While it is boiling add lime juice. Take it off the heat and leave for 15 minutes.

Strain curdled milk through a strainer lined with muslin. Gather up the edges of the cloth and squeeze it to ensure that all liquid has been drained off. The paneer can be used as it is (quite soft) or you can put the paneer in the muslin cloth, in a container, evenly weight the top of the paneer and leave for a couple of hours. This will cause more liquid to be squeezed out and give a firmer product which is better for cutting into cubes and frying.

After surviving the nightmare of Partition the Punjabi attitude to life became very focussed on the immediate. They understood only too well how fickle the hand of fate could be—what one has today may not be here tomorrow so it may as well be enjoyed. As they created a new prosperity for themselves in Delhi they imbued the city with a rough and tumble joie de vivre, and a passion for eating and drinking. The Punjabis were not fussy about their food as long as it was fresh, tasty and plentiful.

The inhabitants of Delhi who had lived there pre-Partition were often aghast at the Punjabi style of eating and cooking. Accustomed to the more refined sensibilities of Delhi's bania and Mughal fare, they were uncomfortable witnessing the unrestrained pleasure with which the Punjabi approached his food and were horrified to see him commit such culinary crimes as eating dal with pulao or eating standing by the roadside.

Punjabi food is arguably at its most authentic in the **dhaba**. These rudimentary food stalls were originally located on major truck routes to provide hearty meals for the truck drivers of India's northern highways (a large number of whom are Punjabis). The robust, earthy and nourishing fare served up in a typical dhaba makes the pallid fried food of Western truck stops look even worse than it is. Protein-rich creamy *dals* made with a variety of lentils and split peas; *paneer dishes*; *curried chicken*; *baingan bharta*; *aloo chholé* and stacks of fresh hot breads such as *roti*, *naan* and *parantha* are the staple diet of North India's highway jockeys (such food is no doubt needed to fortify themselves against the rigours of driving on India's roads). This recipe is for the sort of dal that you would enjoy at a dhaba.

■ *Maa ki dal* ■
Serves 6 (or 3 hungry truck drivers)

Ingredients
1 cup whole black beans (urad)
$^1/_2$ cup red kidney beans (rajma)
1 tsp red chilli powder (or to taste)
1 tbsp minced ginger
8-12 cloves garlic
3 tbsp ghee
4 green chillies, chopped (or to taste)
salt to taste
2 tomatoes, skinned and chopped
2 tbsp cream

Method
Soak beans in 2 litres water overnight or for at least 6 hours.

Drain and rinse beans. Put them in a pan with 2 litres fresh water, add chilli powder and $^1/_2$ tbsp of the ginger, and bring to boil. Boil uncovered for 10 minutes. Reduce heat and continue to simmer beans until almost all the liquid has been absorbed and there is only a small amount left in the pan (enough to stop the beans sticking and to keep them moist). Remove from heat and mash beans until you have a reasonably smooth paste.

While beans are cooking, heat ghee in a frying pan over high heat. Fry remaining ginger and garlic until golden. Add green chillies, salt, tomatoes and $^1/_2$ cup water and cook over medium heat until well amalgamated.

Add this sauce to mashed beans and mix well. Return pan to heat and cook over low heat for 5 minutes, stirring to ensure that it doesn't stick to the base. Add cream and stir through. Serve hot with a pile of roti or bread.

Food this good was not going to remain a trade secret and roadside dhabas are now frequented by all manner of motorists eager to enjoy this hearty fare. Dhabas have also made their way into the city where they provide lunch for much of the city's working population. **Kake-da-Hotel** opposite L block in Connaught Place is a dhaba of legendary status. Every Delhiwallah will have a story of having sought solace/repaired a hangover/ended a big night out or just satisfied serious hunger pangs here. **Express Dhaba** is another popular dhaba located on Delhi's 'Fleet Street'. Earthy, unpretentious dhabas (serving what could well be described as 'North Indian comfort food') such as these have the unique ability to draw people from all of the city's varying backgrounds into one place—it is a phenomenon you are unlikely to see elsewhere in class-conscious Delhi.

If the rugged reality of a genuine dhaba is not to your liking then you might like to enjoy the pleasure of dhaba fare in the gentrified surroundings of the Dhaba restaurant at **Claridges Hotel**. There is a truck, an obligatory tree, charpais, Punjabi music and waiters dressed in typical Punjabi costume—all that is missing is some truck drivers reclining on the charpais chewing paan. The food here is excellent although you will pay noticeably more than you would at a real dhaba. Punjabi food is not all limited to dhabas though, and you can enjoy one of the more refined

Haldiram's, Chandni Chowk

The Rajasthan Stall at Dilli Haat

Chaat and gol gappa at Greater Kailash I

Prince Paan, Greater Kailash I

Dry fruit, nuts and aam papad at a store in Khari Baoli

Pickles and chutneys on display in Khari Baoli

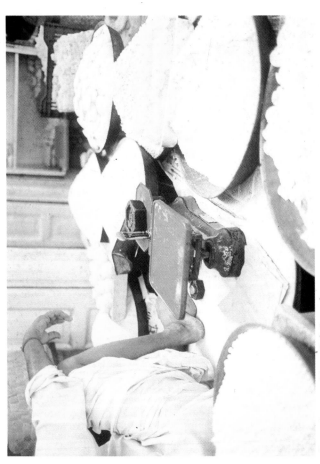

Sugar being sold on Gali Batasha

Fresh vegetables at Chittaranjan Park Market No. 1

Prawns at the fish market in Chittaranjan Park

The fish market, Chittaranjan Park

versions of this cuisine at **Pakwan** at Le Meridian hotel.

A favourite Punjabi food is the *parantha*. The parantha is often mentioned as a food item popularized in Delhi after Partition but this is not entirely correct. The Mughals were know to have enjoyed them. As much time was spent travelling and warring in the Punjab, it is not surprising that they would have become familiar with this Punjabi creation. There were also Punjabis living in Delhi prior to Partition and their pioneering efforts with the parantha were such that by the early decades of the twentieth century Delhi had an established laneway devoted to the production and consumption of paranthas, **Paranthe wale Gali**.

In his autobiography, Patwant Singh describes his boyhood, pre-Partition visits to Paranthe wale gali as 'bliss'.

Parantha wale Gali is a narrow dog-legged lane that links Chandni Chowk to Kinari Bazaar and its main activity is still the production and consumption of paranthas. There are several paranthawallahs in the gali, one of whom claims to have been trading there since 1882. Choose whichever one appeals to you as they will certainly all be trying to attract your custom. The rigmarole is much the same at all. You sit down and a thali with two or three chutneys, pickles and a pile of spiced potatoes on it appears before you. These are to act as condiments to the paranthas and are free of charge (you may ask for them to be replenished). Before long the waiter will bring you your first hot delectable parantha. You pay per piece for the paranthas and they will keep coming to you until you say 'bas'. As they are cooked on an as-needed basis, you may have to wait a few minutes between paranthas but that can only be considered an aid to appetite. The paranthas are stuffed with various fillings—*aloo*, *gobi*, *mooli*, *matar-paneer*, *anardana* (crushed pomegranate seeds), *palak* (spinach) and *papad* (crushed papadam). You can take them as they come or you can request specific fillings. Whatever you decide, paranthas make a satisfying, moorish and very inexpensive snack or meal.

One of the appealing aspects of Delhi for those with culinary interests is that you can quite often watch your food being prepared (I get a little uneasy about watching animals being transformed into meat but it's there if you want to see it). In Paranthe wale Gali you can watch the cook at work as he dexterously makes your paranthas. Perched cross-legged on a raised platform in front of the shop he breaks off a small piece of dough from a larger mound and shapes and rolls the parantha according to the filling; peas are pushed directly into the dough; grated radish is placed between the layers of the dough as it is rolled out. If circumstances prevent you from putting down this book and heading straight for Paranthe wale Gali then these recipes will at least assist you in attempting to replicate what you could be enjoying there.

■ *Parantha* ■
Makes 6

Ingedients
2 cups wholemeal flour (atta)
$^3/_4$-1 cup water
3 tbsp ghee (no substitute), melted
1 tsp salt
ghee for cooking

Method
Sieve flour and salt into a bowl.

Slowly add enough water to form soft dough. Knead for 15 minutes and gradually work in remaining water (you will have to judge how much that is—the dough should be soft but firm and elastic, not sticky). Cover dough with a damp cloth and leave for 30 minutes.

Knead dough lightly again and divide into 6 pieces. Roll out into flat discs about 13 cm in diameter. Spread a little ghee on the surface, fold in half, spread a little more ghee on the surface and fold in half again. Fold it again and press it into a ball. Gently roll out on into a 5 mm-thick disc on a floured surface.

Heat a tava or griddle and place parantha on it. Smear upper side with ghee and drizzle some ghee around edges. Cook for one minute and repeat on other side. Keep turning paranthas and adding ghee until crisp and golden on both sides. Serve hot.

If you wish to add a filling to the paranthas you will need to add it when you are rolling them out. When you have formed the parantha dough back into a ball after spreading it with ghee, press it into a flat disc in your hand. Put a little filling in the centre and work dough around to cover filling completely. Press into a disc and roll out gently. Cook as directed above.

■ Masala Aloo (Spiced Potatoes) ■
Serves 4

Ingredients
1 tbsp ghee or oil
2 tsp cumin seeds
2 tsp minced ginger
6 cloves garlic, crushed
2-3 green chillies finely chopped (or to taste)
salt to taste
1 tsp garam masala powder
1 tsp mango powder (amchur)
1 tsp turmeric powder
$1/2$ tsp red chilli powder (or to taste)
$1/2$ kg potatoes, boiled, peeled and cubed

Method
Heat ghee in heavy-based frying pan. Add cumin seeds and fry until they sputter. Add ginger, garlic, green chillies and salt, and cook until softened. Add garam masala, mango powder, turmeric and chilli powder. Cook for 3 minutes and add potatoes. Add a little water and cook for 5-7 minutes. Gently stir the dish so that the potatoes go a little soft but stay in pieces (it should not all be mush but you want the potatoes to be amalgamated by a little potato mush!)

■ Banana Chutney ■
Serves 6
If you are lucky you will find a banana chutney such as this one accompanying your paranthas.

Ingredients
6 tbsp tamarind
$2^1/2$ cups hot water

3 tbsp brown sugar or jaggery (gur)
1 tbsp minced ginger
$2^1/_2$ tbsp seedless raisins
1 tsp roasted ground cumin seeds
1 tsp mango powder (amchur)
2-3 tsp red chilli powder (or to taste)
3 firm ripe bananas
$^1/_2$ cup melon seeds
salt to taste

Method

Soak tamarind in hot water for 15 minutes. Push water and tamarind through a sieve to extract all the pulp.

Over medium heat cook tamarind pulp, sugar or jaggery, ginger, raisins, cumin, mango powder and chilli powder, until sugar dissolves, water reduces a little and sauce thickens.

Peel and slice bananas thinly and add to sauce. Add melon seeds and salt. Mix well.

Chill before serving.

There are also two small stalls in the gali that specialize in delicate *milk sweets* such as *rabri* and *malai kurchan*. These traditional Delhi sweets are painstaking and time-consuming to make. They are created by boiling milk until it reduces by a third and by slow boiling milk and collecting the skin that forms, a process that takes hours. Both these sweets have a distinctive grainy texture and are truly delectable. Try and resist having that last parantha and save some space for a delicate leaf plate of one of these treats. If your appetite is jaded then take a stroll up and down glittery Kinari Bazaar and see if you can revive it by dodging cows and overloaded rickshaws in this busy thoroughfare.

Punjabis are hearty eaters and the generous portions served at modern Delhi eateries is a legacy of this. Even at five-star hotels (where you would typically find portion sizes decreasing inversely to the amount of money you pay for them), the serving sizes are more than generous. The significant place of Punjabis in Delhi's restaurant and catering industry has meant not only a predominance of Punjabi food in Delhi but also that of 'Punjabiized cuisine' (with the addition of generous doses of tomato, spices and chilli that knock out any subtle or delicate flavours).

The North West Frontier

As Delhi began to gradually settle into the new shape it had taken after Partition, its citizens began to notice that there was more than a sea of new names and faces; there were also new tastes. Before 1947 tandoori food had not been a part of the city's food culture; post 1947 tandoori food had become one of Delhi's foremost culinary passions.

Tandoori food came to Delhi via the Punjab but its origins lie even farther from the city, in the North West Frontier. This mountainous province had played a significant role in India's history. The Aryans in 1500 BC, the Turks, the Mughals and the raiding parties of Shah Alam in the nineteenth century all swept down into India through the North West Frontier. The British had not taken this well-worn route but they kept the area well manned throughout their reign. And when their rule ended, they placed the North West Frontier on the side of the line that said Pakistan. This time it was many of the inhabitants of the North West Frontier who came out of their mountain home into India bringing their traditional oven, the tandoor, with them.

The North West Frontier was—and remains—a sparsely populated area. Many of its inhabitants were required to lead nomadic lifestyles due to the constraints of their professions namely as traders, soldiers and thieves. With the constant threat of invaders and the need to travel great distances on horseback through uncompromising terrain, life in the North West Frontier was one that required stamina and mobility. The criteria for the provision of food was that it needed to be quick, simple and portable; there was little inclination or opportunity for indulging in culinary fripperies but that did not preclude eating well. The dry, rocky terrain did not sustain too many plants that could be eaten. As such *meat* and *milk* were the mainstay of the diet. Animals such as sheep and goats could follow the horses, forage on the available pasture and be slaughtered when required. They also provided milk which could be drunk fresh or turned into *curd*. This could then be used to tenderize and add flavour to the lean animal flesh that the conditions bred.

To cook the meat, the tandoor oven had developed to

suit these conditions. It was portable and could be carried on horseback and its shape (an enclosed box or barrel) meant that it contained heat and allowed for quick cooking. By cutting the meat into small pieces and threading them onto skewers, the tandoor could cook them through in no time. As the tandoor is a covered oven, it had the added advantage of not emitting light or flames that might alert potential enemies (an important consideration in the volatile environment of the North West Frontier). The tandoor was also used for baking *breads*. Simple doughs of flour were mixed up with water and curd and rounds of this dough could be slapped onto the side of the tandoor. (This gave traditional tandoori breads such as naan their characteristic tear-drop shape as they dripped slightly down the side of the tandoor before the heat set them.) Dishes of *lentils* and other *dried legumes* could be cooked by placing them on the top of the tandoor where they stewed slowly (often overnight) courtesy of the contained heat of the oven.

When **Moti Mahal**'s Kundan Lal arrived in Delhi after Partition, as a refugee from the North West Frontier, he could hardly have imagined the culinary juggernaut he was about to launch. Landing in the city with little besides his family and a tandoor, he set about earning a living selling tandoori chicken from a small street stall in Old Delhi. Many of Delhi's new residents would have recognized this style of food and welcomed its familiar flavours; to other Delhiites it was a revelation and they eagerly sought out this new and delicious food. The success of his simple tandoori chicken stall inspired Lal to open Moti Mahal restaurant. His by now legendary *tandoori chicken* remained the draw card, but access to the wide range of foods available in Delhi allowed him to broaden the repertoire of tandoori foods that he could offer in his restaurant. By the late 1960s Moti Mahal was Delhi's most successful restaurant, an essential part of the social fabric for sophisticated Delhiites and international jetsetters. It was during this time that Kundan Lal first introduced many a Westerner to the 'pleasure of eating with one's fingers'. The success of Moti Mahal spawned thousands of imitators and the tandoori dishes that Lal created are now a commonplace in Delhi.

You can still visit Moti Mahal in Old Delhi but its glory days are gone and it is now a somewhat faded rose in appearance. Delhi's glitterati and its attendant 'rent-a-crowd' have all been lured to the south side of the city where the five-star hotels have all opened glamorous restaurants; parking is easier and the sea of humanity does not bear upon you quite so heavily. Despite abandonment by the fashionable crowd and the subsequent lack of need to maintain its appearance, Moti Mahal still attracts a regular and devoted clientele. The reason? The food here is still some of the best in Delhi (it actually creates somewhat of a pleasant juxtaposition to eat such delicious food amongst the diminishing reminders of past glory).

The tandoori dishes at Moti Mahal are expectedly good: *reshmi kabab* (chicken marinated in cream and spices, then coated in besan and cooked in the tandoor) and *bharwan naan* (stuffed with potato and onion) are two standouts on the menu. Kundan Lal is also credited with the invention of *butter chicken* and *chicken pakoras*, both of which you can still enjoy at his restaurant. If a visit to Moti Mahal is not on the cards in your immediate future, you might like to try this version of butter chicken, inspired by the original, which caters to those that don't have access to a tandoor.

■ *Butter Chicken* ■
Serves 4-6

Ingredients
1 cup curd
8 cloves garlic, crushed
2 tbsp minced ginger
2 tbsp lime juice
1 tbsp garam masala powder
1 tsp red chilli powder
1 tbsp vegetable oil
1 kg skinned chicken pieces
1 kg tomatoes, chopped
125 g butter
1 tbsp freshly ground white pepper
2 tsp salt
1 tsp dried fenugreek leaves (kasuri methi)
2 tbsp cream
finely chopped fresh coriander leaves for garnish

Method

Blend curd, garlic, ginger, lime juice, garam masala and oil. Marinate chicken in this for 6 hours.

Thread chicken onto skewers and bake in a tandoor oven until 90% cooked. Or bake chicken in a preheated oven for 15 minutes at 350°F (200°C). Put it aside.

Cook tomatoes over low heat for 10 minutes. Push tomatoes through a sieve (discard seeds and skin).

In a heavy-based frying pan add butter and place over heat. When butter is melted add white pepper, salt, and fenugreek. Add tomato sauce, mix well and put chicken into sauce. Cook for 10 minutes and add cream. Serve hot, garnished with coriander.

If imitation is the sincerest form of flattery then Moti Mahal has been very sincerely flattered as it has inspired a plethora of imitators in Delhi who have copied not only the food but the name. There are quite a few restaurants with versions of the name 'Moti Mahal' in Delhi (which can be confusing), but the original Moti Mahal proudly proclaims on its menus and bills that 'we have no other branch'. You would not be hard pressed to guess then what style of food is served at **Moti Mahal Deluxe**. Of all the imitators, this restaurant probably has the best food. Some Delhiites might tell you that the food here is better than at the original, but this preference for Moti Mahal Deluxe may actually be influenced by more pragmatic factors than the food—it is much easier to park a car here, the decor is more modern, the waiters have cleaner shirts and the person making the comment may never have eaten at

Moti Mahal. Make a meal of their speciality dishes such as *tandoori stuffed potatoes*, *pudina chicken*, *khasta roti* (a cumin-flavoured bread that enjoys a generous coating of butter before being baked) and *tandoori salad*. This skewered salad of green pepper, onion, tomato and paneer is cooked in the tandoor with a liberal basting of salt, cumin, chilli and ghee; the tomatoes just melt in your mouth and it is very hard to stop eating even when satiation point has been reached.

Delhi's most famous restaurant, **Bukhara** (named after the town in the NWF), is also a product of Kundan Lal's North West Frontier culture. Often called the 'best Indian restaurant in the world', Bukhara's dining room is patronized by Delhi's socially prominent citizens and visiting celebrities. Serving sublime North West Frontier cuisine, this restaurant is always busy and has been for its twenty years of operation.

No expense has been spared on making Bukhara as 'frontier' rustic as possible. The rough-hewn stone walls have been hung with a collection of Bukhara rugs and copper cooking vessels. The seating comprises hard wooden stools cut from tree stumps deliberately designed to discourage diners from lingering (there are two busy seatings or batches here at lunch and dinner and demand is such that it sometimes runs to three). The menu comes printed on a slab of lacquered wood (fans of the Flintstones will enjoy this). There are no knives and forks used and it is a 'hands on' experience for everyone: movie stars, captains of industry, politicians and presidents. (Former US President Bill Clinton and his family ate at Bukhara twice during their trip to India in 2000. Clinton later told a US journalist that 'Bukhara had served [him] one of the best meals [he] had had during his eight years in office'.) A large red-and-white-checked bib is supplied to patrons to prevent any unfortunate mishaps with the food which can make the dining room look like an adult nursery! The urbane (and faultless) waiters wear smart khaki kurta-pyjamas and curl-toed joothis. The atmosphere is alluring and warm and those with an inclination for the fanciful can imagine themselves as a spy in a den of political intrigue in the real Bukhara.

The gleaming kitchen is separated from the dining area only by a glass wall and this allows guests to enjoy the theatre of tandoori cooking. Busy chefs continually thread metal skewers with marinated meat, fish, chicken, prawns and vegetables. These are lowered into the tandoor and then rescued with a triumphant flourish at just the right moment. Various bread doughs are patted into rounds and slapped onto the sides of the oven with a padded disc. The Bukhara naan is the size of a small table. When cooked it is dramatically liberated from the tandoor by two chefs with metal skewers, delivered straight onto a platter where it lies, wings upturned, looking like a beached manta and whisked out through the dining room, platter held high, straight to an eager reception at the table (this never fails to turn heads).

The signature dish at Bukhara is the *Sikandri raan* (whole leg of kid) and at least one hundred of these are served daily. Most diners accompany the raan with the *dal makhani Bukhara*. Sceptics will initially recoil at paying Rs 225 for a plate of dal but one mouthful of this silky, rich, smoky flavoured dish is so enticing that apprehension is soon forgotten. The black lentils from which this dal is made (together with spices) are cooked slowly overnight on a tandoor as tradition demands. The dal is then enriched with a generous quantity of butter. Ninety litres of dal makhani Bukhara are devoured everyday in the restaurant and the demand for this dal is so great that it is now sold in cans.

Most diners do not stop at the raan and dal and these two 'staple' items are usually accompanied by dishes such as *tandoori breads, murgh tandoori, tandoori jhinga* (prawns), *tandoori pomfret* and *tandoori phool gobi*. Vegetarians might often feel uninspired about dining at Bukhara when they hear so many waxing lyrical about the raan, but the tandoori phool gobi is worth crossing many oceans for (how's that for waxing lyrical). Here is a recipe inspired by Bukhara's tandoori phool gobi. You will need a tandoor to cook this in to get anywhere near approximating the taste of the dish served at Bukhara.

If you don't have access to a tandoor you might like to try a regular oven or even a barbecue (but it won't be quite the same).

■ *Tandoori Phool Gobi* ■
Serves 6

Ingredients
1 large cauliflower
1 tbsp minced ginger
2 cloves garlic, crushed
$^1/_2$ tsp ajwain
2 tsp red chilli powder
1 tsp turmeric powder
1 cup curd
1 cup gram flour (besan)
salt to taste
pepper to taste

Method
Cut cauliflower into florets. Prick all over with a fork.

Mix all other ingredients together with a fork until smooth. Marinate cauliflower in this sauce for 1 hour.

Thread cauliflower pieces onto skewers and cook in a hot tandoor (if using a regular oven bake on trays at 180°C-200°C) until cauliflower is tender (about 15-20 mins) and coating is golden brown.

Bukhara is one of the most expensive restaurants in Delhi (though you would pay a lot more for the equivalent standard of service, ambience and food in any other major capital around the world) and while the food is unquestionably the best of its kind, you can eat good North West Frontier cuisine at less expense in other locations. After all it is a straightforward style of cuisine that relies on fresh ingredients, robust spicing and well-timed cooking. **Park Balluchi** has a good reputation for its menu of North West Frontier and Afghani specialities. *Paneer tukra* is a delicacy that has found its way onto Park Balluchi's menu from the royal repasts of old Afghanistan. Cubes of paneer are stuffed with groundnuts and spices, marinated in cream and cooked in the tandoor. The *burra gosht Peshawari* (Peshawar is the capital of the NWF) are tender lamb chops marinated in well-spiced sour cream and cooked in the tandoor. Or try the spectacular Park Balluchi showpiece, the *nawati shola*. These kababs of chicken wrapped around fish or lamb (marinated in cream) are served on a flaming sword! Surrounded as it is by the verdant greenery of Hauz Khas Park, it is also one of the most pleasant restaurants to eat at in Delhi.

Corbett's also has a reputation for excellent tandoori food and its unique setting. Named after Jim Corbett, this outdoor restaurant is set up to replicate a jungle camp complete with lush greenery, running stream, fish ponds, tigers, deer and wild boar (of the concrete variety), kerosene lanterns and a tree house. There are also mosquitoes— real ones—like those in a jungle camp. Corbett's is open only in the evenings and only during the cooler months (November through March). It's fun!

City of Refugees II

The influx of refugees into Delhi after Partition created a city where the greater number of residents are not native Delhiites. Whilst Punjabis make up the majority of these newcomers—and it is their culinary habits and preferences that have most shaped the food habits of modern Delhi—there have also been other, smaller, distinct groups of people who have come to reside in Delhi. Many of these people have been refugees arising out of other disturbances in India and the countries that surround her. Washed up in Delhi on the tide of events over which they have had no control, they have sought out the community of their own people and developed ethnically distinct enclaves throughout the city. This, combined with modest numbers, has meant that the culinary habits of these people are only minor elements in the food life of Delhi. That said, there is an exception or two and there is certainly opportunity to explore their cuisines.

Bengal

When Delhi was proclaimed the new capital of India in 1911 a wave of Bengalis began pouring into the city. While technically not refugees born out of any crisis, they were certainly faced with a tough choice. Many of these Bengalis were employed by the government in Calcutta and if they wished to maintain their positions they had little option but to move to Delhi. Others were business people who understood that when the seat of power was moved, the commercial opportunities that would be lost in Calcutta could be recovered in Delhi. Once settled into the city they called for their families to join them and their community grew.

The most obvious evidence of Bengali residency in Delhi is in the proliferation of sweet shops. Bengalis rival Muslims in their addiction to sweetmeats and there has been much culinary effort devoted to the creation of sweet confections in Bengal. While the traditional Muslim sweets of Delhi are based on nuts, dried fruits or rice, traditional Bengali sweets are made from a base of *chhana*.

Chhana is created by curdling milk, then squeezing out the whey through muslin, leaving firm, dry curd. It is thought that the Bengalis learnt this method of making 'cottage cheese' from the Portuguese who began to settle in Bengal in the 1650s. Using chhana as a base, the Bengalis created sweets such as *rasogolla*, *rasomalai* and *sandesh*. Rasogollas are balls of sweetened chhana submerged in a delicate syrup. *Gulab jamun* are similar balls of cottage cheese which have been deep fried and then soaked in a rose-scented syrup. The gulab jamun is said to have been an accidental creation of Shah Jahan's personal chef. *Pantua* and *chhanar jilipi* could be said to be Bengali versions of the gulab jamun. Rasomalai consists of flattened balls of chhana floating in a rich pool of sweetened cream perfumed with cardamom and a sprinkling of pistachio nuts. Sandesh is a distinctive Bengali sweet typically shaped in decorative moulds. It has a soft, fudge-like consistency and a slightly grainy texture. It is the chhana that gives all these sweets their characteristic 'squeaky' texture.

If you want to sample the best Bengali sweets in Delhi then it makes sense to head south to the Bengali suburb of **Chittaranjan Park**. In a quiet local street there you will find one of Delhi's most popular Bengali sweet shops, **Annapurna Mistanna**, but before you launch yourself into an assault on their esteemed sweets, you should consider having lunch or dinner at **Baboo Moshai**. Situated at the C.R. Park-Kalkaji border, this is one of the few places in Delhi where you can sample authentic Bengali food. Until recently Baboo Moshai was not much more than a glorified dhaba but the restaurant's popularity has recently seen it receive a few physical upgrades (air conditioning, more tables, permanent walls).

Ask any Indian to tell you what characterizes Bengali cooking and they will answer, 'fish and mustard oil'. Fish is such a vital part of Bengali cuisine that Bengali Brahmins have always eaten fish (they considered fish to be the fruit of sea). *Hilsa* is a favourite fish in Bengal. It is considered a symbol of fertility and is served at Baboo Moshai bathed in a traditional mustard sauce. Hilsa is a seasonal fish and if it is not available then try a plate of *chingri malai curry* (prawn curry). This curry, rich in coconut milk, has a reputation in Delhi and maintains a loyal following. In keeping with the Bengalis' reputation as fish lovers, there is an excellent fish market in Chittaranjan Park (see chapter 'Where to Shop'). Baboo Moshai has recently added a selection of 'Calcutta Chinese' dishes to the menu. **Banzara** in Chittaranjan Park is a small Bengali resturant that specialises in fish BBQ (after 6 p.m.).

Bananas proliferate in the tropical climate of Bengal and this valuable tree provides bananas, leaves and flowers for culinary purposes. At Baboo Moshai you can try *mochar ghonto* (banana flower cooked in coconut milk with gram and shrimps). This is a light refreshing dish with the banana flower contributing both texture and a delicate flavour. On weekends Baboo Moshai cooks up an unctuous Bengali *chutney*.

■ *Sweet and Sour Tomato Chutney* ■

Serves 10

Ingredients
2 tbsp ghee or oil
$^1/_2$ kg tomatoes, chopped
2 bay leaves
1 tbsp panch phoran (Bengali five-spice mix), ground
1 tsp salt
a pinch of turmeric powder
1 tbsp chopped dates
4 tbsp date palm sugar (nalen gur) chopped*

Method

Heat ghee in a heavy pan. Add tomatoes, bay leaves and panch phoran. Stir for a few minutes. Add salt, turmeric, dates and sugar, stir well and cook for 5 minutes.

Add 1 cup water, cover and simmer over medium heat for 10 minutes.

Serve hot.

*nalen gur is available in Chittaranjan Park market (see chapter 'Where to Shop')

Once you have had you fill of savoury Bengali specialities, you can waddle across to Annapurna Mistanna for some chhanar mishti to cap off your Bengali feast.

If you can't make it to Chittaranjan Park you can still enjoy some of Delhi's finest Bengali sweets. **Annapurna Bhandar** in Chandni Chowk, **Nathu's** and **Bengali Sweet House** in **Bengali Market** and **Evergreen Sweets** in **Green Park** all produce good quality traditional sweets. **Bijoli Grill** at **Dilli Haat** also serves excellent Bengali cuisine.

Kashmir

The verdant green vales and shimmering lakes of Kashmir have meant that it has long been a popular tourist destination. It was the beloved summer playground of the Mughals and the heat-worn Brits took any chance they could to enjoy respite from the plains in the cool climes of Kashmir. For international tourists, one of the highlights of a trip to India used to be a stay on a houseboat on Dal

Lake. Kashmir was also a favourite holiday destination amongst Indians.

Since Partition, Kashmir has been subject to an ongoing territorial war along its Indian-Pakistan border. In the past decade, indiscriminate terrorist attacks in the region have increased. This, combined with the unease created by the war, has virtually dried up the once flourishing Kashmir tourism industry.

Unable to earn a living from tourism, many Kashmiris have come to live in Delhi and they are typically involved in trading the beautiful handicrafts of Kashmir: shawls, papier mâche items and exquisite Kashmiri hand embroidery.

The Mughals procured much of their produce from Kashmir and their regular sojourns there meant that each cuisine drew influences from the other. It is not really possible to pinpoint which way specific influences flowed. Like Mughal food, Kashmiri Muslim food is rich in *ghee*, *spices*, *nuts* and *dry fruit* but there is less emphasis on meat. Kashmiris—Hindu and Muslim—also prefer *lamb* to mutton and lamb is such an integral part of the cuisine that Kashmiri Pandits (Brahmins) eat lamb. The traditional Kashmiri wedding feast is based on lamb cooked in seven different ways. There is a heavy dependence on the lakes of the region to provide *fresh fish* and *vegetables* such as *lotus root*. Kashmiri red chilli powder and turmeric are the spice base for most Kashmiri cooking. *Saffron* is produced in Kashmir and is used extensively in the cuisine as is *mawal* (cockscomb flower).

Unless you know a Kashmiri family, the opportunities to try this rich and splendid cuisine are limited in Delhi. **Chor Bizarre** is one restaurant that has been serving Kashmiri food in Delhi for many years. Here you can dine on *nedr palak* (lotus root cooked with spinach and garlic), *tabak maaz* (lamb ribs that are boiled, then fried and served dry), and *goshtaba* (finely minced young lamb flavoured with cardamom in a yogurt gravy). Goshtaba is traditionally served as part of a Kashmiri *wazwan* (professionally cooked banquet). A traditional wazwan has thirty-six courses, of which up to thirty are meat dishes. If you have the occasion that calls for it you can contact **Ahad Sons** to prepare an authentic wazwan for you (and a significant number of your friends). The Kashmiri family that runs this business is considered to be the best wazwan cooks in India and they cater for all the Kashmiri food fairs throughout the country. If you just want a smaller taste of Kashmir then **Wazwan** at Dilli Haat can fill you up with popular Kashmiri dishes such as goshtaba, *roghan josh* (a chilli-rich lamb curry), and *rista* (meat balls cooked with spinach).

Tibet

When communist China invaded Tibet in 1965, Tibet's spiritual leader, the Dalai Lama, fled and took exile in

India. He was followed there by thousands of Tibetans. Unable to endure the separation from their beloved leader and facing the threat of religious persecution by the Chinese, many of them made an arduous and dangerous journey across the Himalayas to reach India from Tibet. Many devoted Tibetans continue to make this hazardous journey into India to be near the Dalai Lama.

Many of these Tibetan exiles have found their way to Delhi. There they are often to be found engaged in trading—a traditional occupation in their native Tibet—and many of the tourist shops along Janpath are operated by Tibetans. Those not engaged in trading can often be found making and selling Tibetan *momos*.

Momos are steamed or fried stuffed dumplings not dissimilar to the Chinese dim sum. Tibetan momos are far more utilitarian than their Chinese cousins and the delicate and varied fillings of dim sum are replaced with a very basic meat or vegetable filling (a reflection of the limited foods that the arid land of Tibet can produce). The momo is a favourite treat in Tibet and is unfailingly served at a formal meal or celebration. Not surprisingly, momos have found their way onto menus and are a favourite with local populations wherever Tibetans have settled. Delhi is no exception to this and in **Chanakyapuri** there is a string of Tibetan dhabas eager to serve you momos. There is plenty of outdoor seating here and it is a very popular place to enjoy a plate of momos in the evenings. In **Lajpat Nagar Market** at 6.00 p.m. each day, two Tibetan women set up a small stall selling home-made momos. It's best to be there around that time as these momos have somewhat of a reputation in Delhi and are sold out very quickly. Grab a plate and have your fill before setting out to enjoy shopping for bargains in the market. Several stalls at **Dilli Haat** serve good momos: **Momo Mia** and the **Sikkim**, **Mizoram**, **Manipur** and **Nagaland stalls**. Wherever you decide to enjoy some momos, they are always accompanied by a fiery red chilli chutney (this is served separately), and shouldn't cost more than Rs 60-80 a plate. *Thukpa* is a substantial Tibetan noodle soup that is also served at all these places. The soup is full of egg noodles, vegetables and pieces of chicken, mutton or pork and is topped with a generous slurp of green chilli vinegar or red chilli sauce if you should so want. This soup is an inexpensive meal in itself.

The more adventurous might like to head to the Tibetan enclave of **Majnu ka Tila** or **'Chhang Town'** as it is more popularly known. The fluttering prayer flags, maroon-robed monks and boys playing carrom will make you feel as if you have stepped off the Mahatma Gandhi (Ring) Road and into Tibet. Located close to the Interstate Bus Terminal (ISBT), this enclave is popular with students from the Delhi University (North Campus) nearby. Momos and thukpa are plentiful in all the small restaurants here but the repertoire of Tibetan dishes available is broader.

You can try *shaptas* (dry meat preparations), *trimomo* (a steamed bread), *shabaley* (meat-stuffed bread) and *boetuk* (clear soup with small dumplings). If you ask they can usually procure some *chhang* (rice liquor). **Tee Dee**, **Wangdhen House** and **Gyutok** are the most popular restaurants here.

EXPRESS DHABA
Bahadurshah Zafar Marg
(Opposite the Indian
Express building)

DHABA
Claridges Hotel
12 Aurangzeb Road
23010211
1 p.m.-2.30 p.m. &
8-9.30 p.m.

PAKWAN
Hotel Le Meridien
1 Windsor Place
12.30 p.m.-3 p.m. & 7.30
p.m.-Midnight

MOTI MAHAL
Netaji Subhash Marg
23270077
noon-12.30 a.m.

MOTI MAHAL DELUXE
M-30 Greater Kailash I
M-Block Market
New Delhi
26412467, 26410480

12.15 p.m.-3.15 p.m. &
7 p.m.-Midnight

BUKHARA
ITC Maurya Sheraton
Diplomatic Enclave
26112233
12.30-2.45 p.m. (daily)
7.30-11.45 p.m. (Mon, Thu
& Sat)
7.30 a.m.-12.15 a.m.
(Fri & Sun)

PARK BALLUCHI
Inside Deer Park
Hauz Khas Village
26859369
11 a.m.-11 p.m.

CORBETT'S
Claridges Hotel
12 Arungzeb Road
23010211
7 p.m.-11.30 p.m.

BABOO MOSHAI
K-1/52 Chittaranjan Park
26476327, 26215220

12.30 p.m.-3.30 p.m. &
6 p.m.-11.00 p.m.

BIJOLI GRILL
Dilli Haat
(Opposite INA Market)
7 days
10 a.m.-9 p.m.

ANNAPURNA MISTANNA
No 13, DDA Market No. 4
Chittaranjan Park
26412508

NATHU'S & BENGALI
SWEET HOUSE
(see chapter 'Street food,
Snacks and Sweets')

EVERGREEN SWEETS
S-30 Green Park Market
26514646, 26856774

CHOR BIZZARE
Hotel Broadway
Block A 4/15 Asaf Ali Road
23273821
12.00 p.m.-3.30 p.m. &
8.00-11.15 p.m.

AHAD SONS
3A Masjid Moth Village
(Behind Uday Park Market)
26253642, 26256017

WAZWAN
Dilli Haat
7 days
10 a.m.-9 p.m.

TIBETAN DHABAS
Yashwant Place
(Adjacent to Chanakya
cinema)
Chanakypuri
11 a.m.-11 p.m.

CENTRAL MARKET
Lajpat Nagar
(Opposite Archies)
6.00 p.m.-9.00 p.m.

'CHHANG TOWN'
Behing Interstate Bus
Terminus (ISBT)
Mahatma Gandhi (Ring) Road
11 a.m.-9 p.m.

BANZARA RESTAURANT
Shop No. 33, Market No. III
Chittaranjan Park, A-Block
26463062
11 a.m.-11 p.m.

Six

∎

NEIGHBOURS

The broad expanse of northern India abuts several other countries: China, Tibet, Bhutan, Nepal, Pakistan, Bangladesh and Burma. Pakistan and Bangladesh have only been separated from India for a little over fifty years and their shared history means that their cuisines also share a common past. There are distinct culinary differences created by geographical, cultural and economic circumstances but the food of Pakistan and Bangladesh is Indian at heart. China, Nepal and Burma have their own cuisines but these have had little influence on Indian food except in areas where borders are shared. The tightly controlled borders and the self-contained culture of Bhutan have meant little influence in any area has come out of that country. The cuisine of India's neighbouring countries has had no discernible effect on the indigenous food of its capital. Some of these cuisines though, are popular in their own right in the city.

∎ **China**

Chinese pilgrims have been visiting India since the early years of the first millennium AD. Most were Buddhists who came on spiritual quests to the country where the Buddha was born and practised his religion. These pilgrims came on individual journeys and did not enter India to conquer or impose but rather to learn and observe. Chinese merchants also came to India but solely to participate in the lively trade that had existed between the two countries for many centuries (the Delhi Sultans kept Chinese slaves and the Mughal Emperors were much enamoured of Chinese porcelain and Chinese tea).

China and India are home to two of the great cuisines of the world and despite their geographical proximity, neither can be said to have influenced the other. Both countries have their own discrete histories and the food to be found in both places is a consequence of these histories. Nonetheless, Chinese food is very popular in Delhi, albeit typically, an 'Indianized' version of it. 'Chow mein' and 'chop suey' are ubiquitous in fast-food restaurants and street stalls in the city. You probably wouldn't find anything like the Delhi versions of these dishes in China but they suit the local palate. Amongst the numerous restaurants serving that infamous Delhi hybrid Punjabi/Indian Chinese, there are some places that serve the real thing.

The Chinese are discerning eaters and if a Chinese restaurant is full of Chinese people then it can be considered a sure sign that the food is good (obviously this measure can only be applied outside of China). By this reckoning the authentic Cantonese-style food served at **Imperial**

Garden must be very good because Oriental faces often outnumber the Indian ones in the large dining room. Imperial Garden specializes in *fresh seafood* (flown in from India's coastal regions) and are famous for their *mud crab*. On any Sunday the restaurant is always full of people eagerly tackling these unwieldy crustaceans.

The knowledgeable waiters at Imperial Garden are keen to encourage diners to experiment with new tastes, in which they are often successful, but once a new taste is discovered, patrons keep coming back for more of the same. In this way, dishes such as *steamed mushrooms in a crab sauce* and *fresh fish fillet* (seasonal) *with a sauce of soy, garlic and red chillies* have become standards.

Another delicious Chinese tradition you can indulge in in Delhi is *yum cha*. Originally conceived as small snacks to eat while drinking tea, yum cha has developed into a Sunday tradition in Chinatowns around the world. Delhi does not have a large enough Chinese community to have its own Chinatown but you can enjoy a sumptuous yum cha banquet at **Tai Pan** every Sunday. There can be few more pleasant ways to enjoy a lazy Sunday lunch than contemplating the views of Delhi from the silk-swathed nest of Tai Pan while an array of freshly cooked delicate morsels (*dim sum*) keeps appearing. At least eighteen different varieties of dim sum arrive (individually) at the table (served in bamboo steamer baskets); some steamed, some fried, a few boiled, and one or two baked in leaf parcels. The fillings are made variously of minced vegetables, prawns, chicken, bean curd, fruit, and rice. Each dim sum is enjoyed partnered with a distinct dipping sauce or simply bathed in a small dish of soy sauce. (One Indian-Chinese concoction that this writer must confess to being quite fond of is the pungent mustard sauce that appears on the tables of Chinese restaurants in Delhi. Paired with the silky-smooth wrappers of steamed Chinese dumplings, it makes a pleasurable match.) The staff at Tai Pan deliver considered and charming service which adds to the relaxed atmosphere.

The interior at Ichiban does not match the five-star splendour of Tai Pan but the food suffers little for that. The food here retains authentic Chinese flavours but the huge menu does aim to satisfy all tastes and there are some dishes on offer that muddy the waters (anything 'Manchurian' seems to be unique to Delhi not China). Eggplant in hot garlic sauce, spare ribs in honey sauce and a range of bean curd dishes are among the genuine items on offer here. The servings here are more than generous and the prices inexpensive.

Delhiites have been enjoying Chinese food for several decades and there are several Chinese restaurants that have, by the way of their consistency and quality, enjoyed a long and fruitful innings in the city. **Taste of China** and **Fa**

Yian in Connaught Place and **Salt and Pepper** in Greater Kailash I are all established favourites. All three do not mask the flavours of the more delicate Chinese dishes (such as *steamed fish*, my benchmark for assessment) with a heavy dose of chilli and Indian spices. Taste of China serves some unusual Chinese *lotus root* preparations such as *fried lotus root in a spicy chilli sauce* (admittedly this one does have a lot of chilli in it).

The relationship between Delhi and Chinese food is like that of a contented married couple. Currently though, the seemingly unquenchable hot culinary affair in Delhi is with Thai food.

■ Thailand

Burma stands between India and Thailand but Burmese food does not seem to have made an impact on Delhi's food life. The same cannot be said for Thai food. *Seafood and chicken paired with rich coconut milk, lime juice and hot red chillies* are flavours that Delhiites have learnt to love from exposure to South Indian food. Thai food takes these familiar flavours, adds *pungent fish sauce, basil and palm sugar* to create intriguing sweet-sour flavours that Delhiites can't seem to get enough of. New Thai restaurants seem to be opening here every second month and many Chinese restaurants are adding a hefty selection of Thai dishes to their menus.

Delhi's best-known Thai restaurant, **Spice Route** stands out not only for its food but its interior. A Thai-inspired temple has been created within the walls of the Imperial hotel. It took seven years to painstakingly design and execute the restaurant. The bold vibrant colours and the gilded embellishment of the interior of Spice Route certainly make for a memorable eating ambience. The restaurant is divided into sections each with its own style. The wealth section has walls embedded with 24-carat gold leaf. Spice Route is a place that the Mughal emperors would have loved for all its glowing splendour (that is if they could recline on the floor—it is hard to imagine them sitting up at a dining table). Even the animal-shaped napkin rings have been specially crafted for the restaurant. Spice Route is surely one of the most beautiful restaurants in the world.

Spice Route is typically categorized as a Thai restaurant but the menu also features dishes from all the regions that were once part of the colonial 'spice route': Vietnam, Kerala, Malaysia, Sri Lanka, Indonesia and Thailand. The Thai food here is outstanding as are all the other dishes from wherever on the spice route you choose to journey with your taste buds. Try *som tum chae* (tangy raw papaya salad), *tom yum soup* and *hed phad metmamuang* (mushroom and cashew curry) for an inspirational taste of Thailand. You should dress up to visit Spice Route to have any hope of competing with the exquisite interior.

Thai Wok at the Ambavata Complex in Mehrauli is the current darling of Thai food in Delhi. With three Thai chefs in the kitchen and a stunning rooftop terrace with unimpeded views over the Qutub Minar, this restaurant is well worth a visit (or two or three).

You can unwind and enjoy superb Thai food at the **Blue Elephant**. This rooftop restaurant is resplendent with goldfish pond, a jungle of potted palms and well-chosen Thai artefacts. **Baan Thai** also offers patrons opulent surroundings, authentic Thai food (a Thai Master Chef rules the kitchen), and a Thai buffet lunch on weekends.

■ Nepal

Nepal is a tiny landlocked country that shares a border and a religion with India. Like India, the majority of Nepal's population are engaged in agricultural occupations but, unlike India, Nepal does not have numerous large cities where its people can go seeking alternative employment. India and Nepal have an open border and this enables Nepalis to come to India to seek employment. A large number of these Nepalese immigrants head to Delhi, where many of them gain employment as domestic servants. Despite their considerable presence in Delhi you won't find any Nepalese restaurants in the city, but you are very likely to find a Nepalese cook at the helm of many of Delhi's domestic kitchens. Nepalese cuisine shares many similarities with Indian food although it opts for less complicated spice mixes and the flavours are earthier and more straightforward. As I am unable to direct you to a Nepali restaurant I am going to take a few liberties and introduce you to one of my favourite 'Delhi' dishes, *Nepali aloo* (*aloo achar*). As the name suggests, this is a Nepalese dish and it has no connection with real Delhi food but I am going to call it a Delhi dish because that is where I discovered it; It was first served to me by a friend there who had had it made up by her Nepali cook.

■ *Nepali Aloo (Aloo Achar)* ■
Serves 4 as side dish

Ingredients
2 medium potatoes
$^1/_2$ cup sesame seeds
2 tbsp oil (mustard oil is best)
$^1/_2$ tsp fenugreek seeds
$^1/_2$ tsp turmeric powder
$^1/_2$ tsp salt
$^1/_2$ tsp chilli powder
1 tsp mango powder (amchur)*
juice of 1 lime

Method
Boil or steam potatoes, skin and cut into pieces.

Toast sesame seeds in a dry frying pan until golden. Grind sesame seeds in a blender until they become a fine powder.

Heat oil in frying pan and fry fenugreek seeds until they sputter, add turmeric and salt and cook for 30 seconds.

Add contents of pan to ground sesame seeds and stir in mango powder and lime juice. Mix to a paste, adding more lime juice or water if necessary.

Mix sesame paste into chopped potatoes.

*if mango powder is unavailable you can use more lime juice.

IMPERIAL GARDEN
E-3 Local Shopping Centre
Masjid Moth GK-II
26437288/90/91
12 p.m.-3 p.m. &
7 p.m.-11 p.m.

TAI PAN
The Oberoi
Dr Zakir Hussain Marg
24633030
Sunday Yum Cha Brunch
12.30 p.m.-2.45 p.m.

ICHIBAN
9 Pandara Road Market
23386689, 23386599

TASTE OF CHINA
N-18 Connaught Place
New Delhi
23730279
11 a.m.-11 p.m.

FA YIAN
A-Block 25/5 Middle Circle
Connaught Place
23323272, 23233237
11 a.m.-3.30 p.m. &
6.30 p.m.-11 p.m.

SALT & PEPPER
M-58 Greater Kailash Mkt-1
26417796, 26223076
12.30 p.m.-3.30 p.m. &
7.30 p.m.-11.30 p.m.

SPICE ROUTE
Hotel Imperial
Janpath
23345678
12.30 p.m.-2.45 p.m. &
7.30 p.m.-10.45 p.m.

BLUE ELEPHANT
The Intercontinetal
15 Barakhamba Avenue
23411001

12.30 p.m.-3 p.m. &
7.30 p.m.-Midnight

BAAN THAI
The Oberoi
Dr Zakir Hussain Marg
24633030
12.30 p.m.-3.30 p.m. &
7.30 p.m.-11.30 p.m.

THAI WOK
1091/1 Ambavata Complex
Mehrauli
26644289
12 p.m.-3 p.m. &
8 p.m.-11 p.m.

∎

Seven

REGIONAL CUISINE IN DELHI

The country we see marked on our modern maps as India is a British creation. Prior to colonization by the British, India had not been a 'country'; it was a subcontinental land mass that was broken up into numerous independent kingdoms and principalities. These differed greatly in size but each had its own ruler, unique language, distinct culture and its own cuisine. Religion and geography created commonalities between some kingdoms but also contributed most significantly to differences with others. The fortunes of war also dictated the influences that these kingdoms came under. A Hindu principality could suddenly find itself ruled by Muslims and then just as suddenly find itself returned to Hindu rule—rulers and boundaries were constantly evolving.

When the British united India into one country they sub-divided her into twenty-five states. The shape each state took on the map of India was often decided by the boundaries of these earlier independent kingdoms. This meant that the majority of the Indian states retained their cultural uniqueness. Today there are, besides the official languages of Hindi and English, fourteen Indian languages recognized by the Indian Constitution. There are also another 1300 dialects spoken amongst India's widely heterogeneous population.

This variance in language in India has its counterpart in the variance amongst cuisines throughout the country. You could divide India into north, south, east and west, then into states, then into regions within states and then into discrete communites and each would have its own distinctive cuisine.

It is only fitting that the capital of India should showcase these unique regional cuisines.

■ Dilli Haat

The best place to begin an exploration of Delhi's regional food offerings is at **Dilli Haat**. An initiative of the Delhi government and Delhi Tourism, the concept of Dilli Haat was inspired by the district melas or fairs that are held all over India. Unlike traditional melas which are by their nature temporary affairs, Dilli Haat is a permanent fixture.

The offerings at Dilli Haat are twofold. The forecourt of this open-air market is filled with stalls selling a range of Indian crafts. Originally conceived of for the tourist market, Dilli Haat has become a fashionable spot for Delhiites to search for unique inexpensive items with which to decorate their homes. Dilli Haat is also a favourite spot for a quick snack or meal.

At the rear of the market you will find a collection of dhabas that offer cuisines from all the states of India. There are also stalls selling ice-cream, drinks and other generic food items.

Do not go expecting to find the haute cuisine of these states, as the offerings at Dilli Haat can lean towards the fast-food side. There is also a similarity between the menus of many of the stalls. After a visit to Dilli Haat you could be forgiven for thinking that Tibetan *momos* were the national Indian dish given the number of 'regional' stalls that serve them.

The quality of the food served at the stalls varies but **Bijoli Grill** (Bengal), **Anantha** (Kerala), **Rajasthan**, and **Sports** (Lakshwadeep) are all consistent in their output. Grab a chilled *tender coconut water* and some *Lakshwadeep samosas* (filled with cabbage and black mustard seeds) and peruse the market. Alternatively you could avail of the outdoor seating. There are also regular regional festivals held at Dilli Haat. The Delhi Tourism Authority can provide details of the programmes on offer.

■ State Bhavans

Each state of India has a **bhavan** (house) located in Delhi. These bhavans serve several functions: they are offices for the business that each state conducts in the capital;

they are the state tourist offices in the capital and provide accommodation and support for those visiting Delhi from that particular state. Many of these state bhavans also have canteens to provide meals for the office workers and bhavan guests.

Whilst in other offices workers usually have to be content with homogeneous canteen fare, the workers of Delhi's state bhavans have their own cuisine served to them. Typically the food served is the everyday fare of that state. A quick and inexpensive meal is available to workers and visitors. But that doesn't mean it isn't good food— after all, Indians are fairly particular about what they eat.

Some state bhavans such as that of **Tamil Nadu** do not serve meals to outside guests but you can follow the queue of office workers and Delhiites alike through the maze of buildings that form the **Andhra Bhavan** and onto some appetizing food in the canteen.

This large canteen is light, clean and run with a military-like efficiency. You buy a meal coupon at the front counter and take a seat at one of the communal tables. A waiter very quickly brings you a thali. On it you will find *dal, three vegetable dishes* (one of which will always be potato), *two spicy chutneys, rice, papads, puris, curd* and a *sweet* (often a rich semolina *halwa*). All this costs a meagre Rs 80, and the food is potentially never-ending. A waiter comes around ladling out refills of the dishes until you tell him to stop. You can order additional dishes of chicken or mutton for a further Rs 50 if you need to add some flesh to this vegetarian meal.

Andhra Pradesh is renowned for the use of red hot chillies in its cuisine and the food here is no exception (don't worry if you are not a chilli aficionado; not all the dishes are hot and you can always use the curd to cool it down). This is not really a place to linger as the turnover is brisk but it is definitely worth a visit if business takes you to the area. It is also a good place to bring children as the meal comes quickly and there is no fuss.

Other state bhavans that serve meals to outside guests are those belonging to **Gujarat**, **Karnataka**, **Jammu and Kashmir**, **Orissa**, **Goa**, **New Sikkim House** and **Bihar**.

State bhavans do not offer a high-class dining experience but they do offer a realistic insight into the daily eating habits of ordinary Indians. This culinary experience also provides a nice counter to the more elaborate royal or special-occasion food typically served in Delhi's regional restaurants.

■ Royal Rampur Cuisine

If the simple offerings of the state bhavans have left you feeling virtuous, you can make up the calories you didn't consume there by paying a visit to the **Rampur Kitchen**. This restaurant specializes in the elaborate cuisine of the Nawabs of Rampur.

The Nawabs of Rampur were originally Rohillas (brigands) whom the British had been unable to subdue despite their best efforts. Realizing that force was not going to work, the British made them Nawabs (rulers) and granted them sizeable and fertile tracts of land around Rampur (in Uttar Pradesh). This plan worked and the new Nawabs began to spend their now considerable wealth on living a grand life (which left them too busy to bother the British). They became well known for their ostentatious tastes, for the Rampur Hound that they bred and for the rich, elaborate cuisine that they enjoyed.

All this glory eventually wound to its inevitable conclusion and Rampur is now just another nondescript town on the main train line between Delhi and Varanasi. You can catch a brief glimpse of the Nawab's ornamental train siding (now crumbling) when you pass through Rampur but the Nawab is long gone. Rampuri cuisine has not faded out with the Nawabs though—the roadside kababs in Rampur remain hyperbole-inspiring.

The cuisine enjoyed by the Nawabs of Rampur is very similar to Mughal food. (The Nawab of Rampur was one of the Muslim rulers who welcomed the royal cooks from Delhi when the British expelled the Muslims from the city after the Mutiny.) It would be unlikely that the inexperienced diner could tell them apart. Rampuri food distinguishes itself though by *unique masalas* devised in the Nawab's kitchens. To familiarize yourself with these unique flavours you can partake of a distinctly Rampuri menu.

Before you start to eat, refresh your palate with a subtly spiced *Rampuri nimbu pani*. Then launch into the *shami kabab Rampuri* and the *dal Rampuri*. As you are sampling royal Muslim fare, you must finish up with something sweet. So have a dish of *Rampur ki sevian* (vermicelli cooked in sugar and garnished with khoya and pistachios).

■ South India

'All roads lead to Delhi' is a centuries-old saying but it has only been a few decades since there have been decent road connections between the northern and southern halves of India. Once the connections were made, the South came right on up to the North and landed in Delhi with a culinary bang.

South Indian food is second only to tandoori food in its proliferation on menus in Delhi. South Indian snacks such as *masala dosa*, *idli* and *vada* are available in numerous sweetshops, fast-food joints, restaurants and hotels throughout the city.

For sixteen years Delhi's most popular South Indian culinary palace has been **Sagar**. This wasn't the first restaurant to serve South Indian food to Delhiites but it was in the vanguard. Sagar opens for breakfast at 8.00 a.m. and finishes up at 11.00 p.m. and there are very few times in that long day where there is a lull in people coming through the door. Queues are typical here on weekends although the turnover is quick, so you don't have to wait long. Sagar's masala dosa is legendary. The dosa is light and crisp, the slightly sour taste (the batter for the dosa is fermented overnight) perfectly counters the spicy potato filling. It is unusual if the first customer of the day does not order a plate of *idli-sambar*. Sagar's idlis are fluffy and feather-weight, the tangy, spiced sambar is thickened with dal to create just the right consistency to cling lightly to the idli. Sagar's *rava kesan* is a South Indian pudding made from semolina, ghee, nuts and spices; the ingredients and the style of cooking are little different from the traditional halwas of Delhi but the heady spicing creates a pudding that is redolent of a rich fruit-filled Christmas cake. Sagar has eight branches throughout Delhi.

The type of food served at Sagar is *Udipi food*. This completely *vegetarian* food is derived from the Brahmanical temple food of South India. It spread out all over the country because it was considered safe to eat by those Southerners who were travelling. The prolific spread of this style of vegetarian food has contributed to fostering the impression that South Indian food is entirely vegetarian. In reality the northern states of India actually have a much higher percentage of vegetarians than the southern ones. Only six per cent of the population of Kerala and twenty-one per cent of Tamil Nadu's population are vegetarian. These figures are arrived at not because South Indians are great meat eaters but because *fish* and *seafood* are an integral part of their lives.

There are a multitude of communities in South India that eke out their livelihood, and most of their daily food, fishing along the long coastlines of their ocean-bordered states. The fish and seafood they catch is combined with ingredients such as *coconut milk*, *black mustard seeds*, *curry leaves*, *red chillies* and *tamarind* to create another distinctive style of South Indian food.

Delhi has not been a city with a traditional passion for fish and seafood. Before it became a wide ribbon of sludge, the Yamuna supplied fish to the city but it was only considered safe to eat this fish during the cooler months of the year. Situated thousands of miles from any ocean, Delhi's citizens would have had little opportunity to enjoy the largesse of the ocean. (The Mughal Emperors made much ceremony out of their first—and often only— sighting of the ocean.) With the development of fast, modern freight services, fresh fish and seafood now arrive daily in Delhi from all over the country and Delhiites are making up for lost time with a vengeance. Seafood has become incredibly popular and the South Indian styles of seafood are the most appealing. **Keraleeyam** is a little restaurant nestled in the shadows of the Indian Oil Bhavan. During the day it serves lunch to numerous office workers; in the evenings it is full of local residents. The speciality here is *appam*, a lacy coconut pancake that takes on the shape of the kadhai it is cooked in. It is the perfect accompaniment to *nadan meen curry* (a tamarind-based fish curry), *chemmeen masala* (shrimps in a thick spice paste) or *meen molly* (a Goan-inspired fish curry flavoured with vinegar). Instead of a knife and fork (available if needed), you break off a piece of the crisp-edged appam and scoop up the rich curry with it. The bottom of the appam is thick, soft and spongy, ideal for sopping up the rich gravy at the bottom of the dish. Aside from seafood, Keraleeyam offers fiery *Chettinad chicken* (cooked in a thick pepper sauce), a traditional dish of the Chettinad trading community of Tamil Nadu. Finish your meal with *pineapple halwa* and fresh *Mysore-style coffee* (coffee is the drink of the South, tea the drink of the North).

The food at Keraleeyam is as good as any of the more expensive South Indian restaurants, but this is not a fancy place. The linoleum floor is scuffed and worn and the walls need a good coat of paint. If you feel this might dull your appetite then you can order takeaway.

Coconut Grove has been attracting a constant stream of hungry customers for many years now. They come here to here to dine on *appams* and *stew, konju biryani* (prawn biryani, a southern take on a northern classic), *chemmeen thoran* (shrimp cooked dry with grated coconut, curry leaves, red chilllies and black mustard seeds and *kalan* (yam and raw banana cooked in seasoned thick yogurt gravy). Customers who like something sweet to round off a spice-infused meal always leave room for their *ada prathaman* (pounded rice batter cooked in banana leaves which is then simmered in jaggery, coconut milk, nuts and dry fruit). Meals here are accompanied with *chilled coconut milk* straight from the coconut or *black coffee flavoured with palm sugar*. Coconut Grove also serves *brown rice* (somewhat of a rarity in North India).

Just a few kilometres past the Qutab Minar in a lush green hollow you will find **Royal Dakshin**. This beautiful restaurant has the serenity of a temple and an air of calm pervades (after negotiating your way through the hecklers at the Qutab Minar car park, this peace is especially welcome). The tasteful decor is matched by attentive professional service and exceptional food. The South Indian food served at Royal Dakshin is rich and full of complex flavours that both tease and satisfy the taste buds; it is a style of food considered to have developed in reaction to the Brahmanical restraint with food that has influenced so much of South India.

The Brahmins thought that the use of too many spices would arouse the passions, but let passions be ignited if you choose to eat at Royal Dakshin. *Fish kaithili* (fish marinated in poppy seeds), *kozhi varthiyathu* (chicken with aniseed), *chemeen curry* (prawn curry) are all 'arousing' choices. There is also a selection of *lamb* and *mutton* dishes on the menu—the Brahmins would be aghast! (Royal

Dakshin also makes the perfect place for a romantic candlelit dinner.)

Swagath is the latest venture from the Sagar chain but there is no *masala dosa* on the menu. The menu at Swagath is wide-ranging but the dishes to take note of are the *seafood* dishes from Mangalore. Fresh seasonal *fish*, *prawns* (small, king, jumbo) and *crab* are all offered in a variety of Mangalorian-style sauces. The seafood cooking of Mangalore has all the components identified with South Indian seafood cooking (coconut milk, black mustard seeds, curry leaves) but these are combined with a generous infusion of the spices more typically associated with North Indian cooking (turmeric, cumin, coriander). Swagath is a more upmarket restaurant than its vegetarian siblings and the light-filled dining room is a pleasant place to enjoy a leisurely seafood meal.

■ Regional Food II

As the regional food of India rides a mounting wave of popularity and interest both in India and in the West, more regional restaurants will appear in Delhi. In the meantime, most of Delhi's big hotels offer food festivals that highlight for a short period a specific cuisine or style of cooking from around India. You will find these festivals listed in the 'dining out' and 'events pages' of local Delhi publications. (A list of these publications appear at the end of the chapter 'Delhi: The Modern City'.)

DILLI HAAT
Aurobindo Marg
(Opposite INA Market)
10 a.m.-9 p.m.

ANDHRA PRADESH BHAVAN
1 Ashoka Road
23382031
Breakfast 8.30 a.m.-10.30 a.m.
12 p.m.-3 p.m. &
7.30 p.m.-10 p.m.

THE RAMPUR KITCHEN
8A Khan Market
New Delhi
24631222, 24603366
12.30 p.m.-3.30 p.m. &
7 p.m.-11 p.m.
(there is also a branch in
GK II)

SAGAR
18 Defence Colony Market
24621451
8 a.m.-11 p.m.

COCONUT GROVE
Hotel Indraprastha
19 Ashoka Road
23368553
Noon-3 p.m. & 7 p.m.-11 p.m.

ROYAL DAKSHIN
DDA Picnic Huts
(Near Andheria Mor)
Mehrauli
26567701
12.30 p.m.-3.30 p.m. &
7.30 p.m.-11.30 p.m.

KERALEEYAM
60/2 Yusuf Sarai
(Opposite Indian Oil Bhavan)
26527512
11 a.m.-11 p.m.

SWAGATH
14 Defence Colony Market
24654537, 24654538
11 a.m.-12 a.m.

■

Eight

FESTIVALS

If any proof was required that modern Delhi is a truly secular city then the list of festivals that the city celebrates should provide all the evidence needed. The festivals of Holi, Dusshera and Diwali are celebrated throughout the city. Id-ul-Fitr, Mahavira Jayanti, Muharram, Christmas and Easter are festivals celebrated predominantly by their respective communities within the city.

And what would a festival be if it wasn't accompanied by some special foods?

■ Holi

Spring is a very brief season in Delhi. It arrives late February and by late March the summer heat is beginning to build. But its arrival is celebrated every year with the riotous festival of Holi.

The legend of Holi celebrates the triumph of Lord Krishna over the demon ogress, Holika. She had been sent to burn down Krishna's house but he strategically turned the tables and Holika was burnt to death instead.

On the eve of Holi, bonfires are built to symbolize the burning of Holika and the triumph of good over evil.

The origins of many Indian festivals are tied to the eternal cycle of the seasons and the harvest, and Holi is no exception. It falls on the full moon at the time of year when the wheat harvest is being brought in. The hard work has been done, some money has been made; it is time to celebrate.

On the day of Holi all social conventions are dispensed with from dawn until noon and people play Holi by squirting coloured water and throwing coloured powders at each other. A few weeks before Holi, stainless steel dishes filled with pyramids of lurid-coloured powders start appearing at the markets around Delhi. Enthusiastic youngsters encourage their parents to buy this powder early, hoping that they may be able to indulge in playing Holi before the actual day. This does not usually happen and they are confined to practising for the big day by throwing plain water balloons at passers-by from the safety of their apartment balconies.

You are faced with two choices on Holi—you hide or you become an unrecognizable multicoloured creature. As a Westerner, I had represented an irresistible target for water balloons prior to Holi; on Holi I was a prime target for the real thing. As the doors opened on the lift in my apartment building, I found myself under siege from boys wielding the latest high-technology, pump-action water guns filled with purple and pink dye (fortunately, as instructed, I had worn old clothes). The chowkidar was more restrained and asked if he could play holi with me. He rubbed some green powder into my hair. I then faced another well-armed posse of large and small children. Half an hour later I was a walking rainbow. It took days to get rid of all the colour from my person.

This scene is enacted all over the city, often accompanied by the banging of drums, building up to a good-humoured midday climax wherever crowds have gathered to play Holi. The mellow mood of Holi participants is traditionally maintained by a small intake of *bhaang* (cannabis) either in a sweet drink or a savoury nibble.

■ *Bhaang Thandai* ■
Serves 4
You can make this recipe without the bhaang for those who would rather keep their wits about them.

Ingredients
1 tbsp almonds
1 tbsp pistachio nuts
$^1/_2$ tbsp poppy seeds
4 green cardamoms
1 tsp black peppercorns
$^1/_4$ cup rose petals (fresh or dried) or
1 tbsp rose water
1 tbsp bhaang seeds
1 litre milk
1 cup sugar

Method

Soak all dry ingredients (except sugar) in $^1/_2$ litre water for 2 hours.

Grind all ingredients to a fine paste, either by hand in a mortar and pestle or in a food processor.

Place a layer of muslin cloth over a sieve or use a very fine sieve. Place sieve over a sturdy bowl. Using the back of a spoon push mixture through the sieve to extract as much liquid as possible. Keep on pressing mix with the spoon until it becomes dry and husk like.

Discard residue in sieve and add strained liquid to milk along with sugar and rose water (if used).

Stir well to dissolve sugar.

Serve well chilled.

■ *Bhaang ki Pakode* ■
Makes 12 pieces

Ingredients
1 cup gram flour (besan)
2 tsp salt
$^1/_2$ tsp soda bicarbonate
$^1/_2$ tsp turmeric powder
$^1/_2$ tsp red chilli powder
$^1/_2$ tsp ajwain
1 tsp pomegranate seed powder or mango powder (amchur)
1 onion, cut into thin rounds
1 potato, cut into thin slices
1 tbsp ground bhaang seeds
oil or ghee for deep frying

Method
Sift flour, salt, soda bicarbonate and spice powders into a bowl.
Add enough water to make a batter of dropping consistency.

Mix onion, potato and cannabis seeds into batter.

Heat ghee or oil in a kadhai, wok or deep pan over medium heat until hot.

Drop spoonfuls of batter into hot oil and fry until golden. Remove with a slotted spoon and drain on kitchen paper.

Serve hot with green chutney

In the days leading up to Holi, it is traditional for houses to be spring cleaned and for the women of the house to prepare special Holi sweets called *gujjia* (or *gooja*). Each family will have their own recipe for gujjia and some now use a press to shape the sweets. All the sweetshops in Delhi will have a tray piled high with gujjia on their counter during Holi.

■ *Gujjia* ■
Makes 20 pieces

Ingredients
500 g plain flour (maida)
$1/2$ cup ghee
1 cup semolina
500 g khoya (dried unsweetened condensed milk), grated
1 cup fine sugar
$1/2$ cup flaked almonds
$1/2$ cup seedless raisins, chopped
2 tbsp chironji seeds, chopped
1 tsp aniseed, crushed
$1/2$ cup grated coconut
oil or ghee for frying

Method

Sieve flour and add $^1/_2$ cup ghee. Rub ghee into flour and add enough cold water to form a soft dough. Knead dough until smooth, cover with a damp cloth and keep aside.

Toast semolina in a dry kadhai until golden, add khoya and keep stirring. Mix in sugar and add almonds, raisins, chironji, aniseed and coconut. Cool to room temperature.

Divide dough into 20 small balls. Roll each ball into a circle about the size of a saucer. Place a spoon of semolina mix on half the circle and brush edges with water. Fold top of dough over filling and seal edges. Crimp edges with a fork.

Heat ghee or oil in a kadhai over medium heat. Fry gujjia until golden. Remove from oil with a slotted spoon and drain on kitchen paper. Cool and store in an airtight container.

■ Muharram

In the first month of the Muslim lunar calendar, the Muslim festival of Muharram is celebrated in Delhi. This ten-day festival is celebrated by Shia Muslims. The festival commemorates the martyrdom of the Prophet Mohammad's grandson, Iman Hussain. For nine days devotees decorate tazias (replicas of Iman Hussain's tomb). On the tenth day these replicas are carried in processions through the streets of Delhi (most notably in Old Delhi and the area around the Nizamuddin dargah). Emotionally charged devotees wail and beat their chests as they carry the tazias. To identity with the martyred Hussain some will whip themselves or create self-inflicted wounds. The street procession is for men only, the women complete their worship at home. There are also passion plays and readings from the life of Hussain in mosques during this festival.

A family feast concludes the day. The meat and wheat dish called *haleem* is a traditional dish at Muharram feasts and no Muslim festival can be allowed to pass without a celebratory *sweet dish*.

■ *Haleem* ■
Serve 4-6

Ingredients
1 cup cracked wheat (dalia)
$^1/_2$ cup husked Bengal gram (chana dal)
500 g mutton, diced
1 tbsp minced ginger
4 cloves garlic crushed
3 green chillies, minced
200 g ghee or butter
2 onions, finely sliced
1 tsp turmeric powder
2 tsp garam masala powder
salt to taste
8-10 cups water
2 tbsp lime juice
fresh mint leaves for garnish

Method
Soak wheat overnight.

Soak dal for 1 hour.

Mix mutton with half the ginger, garlic, and green chillies and leave to marinate for an hour.

Heat half the ghee and fry onions until crisp and golden. Drain on kitchen paper.

Add remaining ginger, garlic and chillies to ghee and fry

for a few minutes. Add drained wheat, dal, turmeric, garam masala, marinated mutton and salt. Add water and cook until all the liquid is absorbed and meat is tender. Take off the fire and mash cooked mixture. Return to fire and let cook for 10-15 minutes.

Put haleem into serving dish. Melt remaining ghee and pour it over meat, sprinkle lime juice over the top, followed by fried onion and mint leaves.

■ *Sheer Khurma (vermicelli cooked in milk)* ■
from: The Essential Delhi Cookbook
Serves 15

Ingredients
$2^1/_2$ litres milk
$1/_4$ cup ghee
50 g fine vermicelli
$1/_2$ cup khoya (dried unsweetened condensed milk)
5 tbsp chironji
4 tbsp sultanas or kishmish
$1/_3$ cup slivered almonds
500 g sugar
a few drops of kewra essence

Method
In a large pan bring milk to a boil, reduce heat and simmer for 15-20 minutes until slightly thickened.

Heat ghee in a kadhai or wok and fry vermicelli until golden.

Drain vermicelli and put into milk along with khoya, chironji, sultanas and almonds. Cook for 15-20 minutes more, stirring frequently until thick and creamy.

Remove from heat. Add sugar and stir until dissolved. Stir in kewra essence.

Chill and serve.

■ Easter

Like Holi, the dates for the Christian celebration of Easter are determined according to the full moon. This means that these two festivals often fall around the same time of the year. Delhi's Christian population is small and Easter celebrations tend to be overshadowed by the Holi festivities. There are church services, prayers and hymns at the city's churches during Easter week and European-style bakeries stock decorated *chocolate* and *sugar Easter eggs* and *hot-cross buns*.

■ Mahavir Jayanti

On 25 April, Delhi's Jain community gathers at the Lal Mandir Digambar Temple in Chandni Chowk to celebrate the birth of the Vardhamana Mahavira, the founder of the Jain religion, who was born on this day 2500 years ago. The temple is brightly lit and decorated and devotees begin coming to the temple well before dawn. A procession is held in Chandni Chowk and worshippers carry huge cut-outs of the Mahavira and tableaux depicting the effects of social evils (as interpreted by the Jains). Vegetarianism is one of the strongest tenets of Jainism and the celebratory dishes served on this day must meet all the Jain dietary directives.

■ Navratra

'Navratra' means 'nine nights' and there are two Navratras in Delhi during the year. The first one begins around the start of the Hindu New Year on April 12 (this date varies throughout the country but it will always be around this date); the second Navratra concedes with Dusshera or Durga Puja. During the Navratra, devotees complete a prescribed cycle of pujas and observe a fast.

Those observing the Navratra fast eat *phalahaar* (literally 'fruit meal'), or non-cereal food. This means that no lentils or grains are eaten; the food is completely vegetarian, and chemically processed salt, hing, turmeric and amchur are not to be used. Only one meal a day is eaten but *fruit* and *milk products* can be freely consumed. Most restaurants in Delhi offer special Navratra dishes during this time and fruit stalls enjoy a busier than usual trade. There is also a strong demand for 'permitted' milk-based delicacies such as *kulfi*, *rabri*, *kheer* and *lassi* (some fast that!).

Singhara (water chestnut) is a starchy vegetable that is used extensively during Navratra as a substitute for grains in breads and puddings.

■ *Singhare ki Roti (Water chestnut Roti)* ■
Makes about 10 rotis

Ingredients
1 cup water chestnut flour (singhare ki atta)
1 tsp rock salt (lohri namak)
1 cup water
ghee for frying

Method

Sift flour and salt together.

Add water gradually and blend well to make a thick pouring batter.

Heat a tava or a heavy-based frying pan and rub a little ghee on it.

Gradually pour a ladle of batter onto tava. Spread batter evenly.

When bubbles appear in the roti rub a little ghee on the top and turn over.

When blackish brown on both sides it is cooked. Remove and serve hot.

■ *Singhare ka Halwa* ■
Serves 6

Ingredients
1 cup sugar
$4^1/_2$ cups water
6 tbsp ghee
1 cup water chestnut flour (singhare ki atta)
seeds of 1 green cardamom, crushed
1 tbsp slivered roasted almonds

Method

Add sugar and water to a pan and cook over a medium heat until sugar is dissolved. Keep on the simmer.

Melt ghee in another pan, add flour and stir over medium heat. Cook until ghee is absorbed and flour golden.

Add simmering sugar syrup and cardamom and bring to boil. Lower heat and simmer until liquid is absorbed.

At this stage, you can stir occasionally. A thin line of melted ghee will form around the edges when it is ready. This should take 5-7 minutes.

Serve hot garnished with almonds.

■ Mango Festival

During the hottest months of the year, there are few festivals in Delhi. It is just too hot for people to summon much enthusiasm for anything—except mangoes! In July each year, the Delhi Tourism Development Corporation hosts an annual mango fair. There are typically about 200 of India's 1100 mango varieties on display here and you can taste them all (if you have the energy). There are also other mango products such as *drinks*, *ice-creams* and *chutneys* available and a competition is held for the best mango recipes. Despite the soaring July temperatures this fair always draws large crowds of mango devotees, who leave sticky but satiated.

One way to cope with summer heat in Delhi is to eat lots of chilled mangoes and mango ice-cream.

■ *Mango Ice-cream* ■
Serves 4-6

Ingredients
1 litre milk
1 cup mango pulp
1 cup sugar

Method
Bring milk to boil in a heavy-based pan. Cook until reduced by a third. Add sugar and cook until dissolved. Mix in mango pulp.

Cool and freeze in trays or put through an ice-cream churn.

■ Dusshera/Durga Puja

Dusshera celebrates the victory of Lord Ram over the demon, Ravana. Ravana had captured Ram's wife Sita and taken her to his island kingdom of Lanka. After many years of battle Ram defeat the demon and rescued his beloved Sita. In Delhi, Dusshera is celebrated over ten days with re-enactments of stories from the *Ramayana*. On the tenth night, giant effigies, filled with fire crackers of Ravana, his brother Kumbhakaran, and his son Meghnad, are burnt throughout the city.

Durga Puja is held concurrently with Dusshera. Durga Puja celebrates the victory of the goddess Durga over her enemy Mahisasura, the buffalo-demon. The gods worshipped are different but both these festivals celebrate the victory of good over evil. The Navratras are an inseparable part of both these festivals.

Durga Puja is the most important festival of the year for Delhi's Bengalis, and the streets of Delhi's Bengali-dominated areas take on a carnival atmosphere during this time. The star attraction at these celebrations are the temporary pandals which house the images of Durga and her family. These pandals are often masterly replicas of buildings such as the Taj Mahal that have been crafted out of canvas, bamboo and polystyrene foam. Side shows, entertainment and food stalls surround these pandals and the activities—both religious and secular—go on late into the night.

At the conclusion of the festival, the effigies of Durga are taken to the Yamuna where they are thrown into the water. In throwing the goddess to the river, all feelings of hostility, anger and envy are meant to be discarded.

At the conclusion of Durga Puja, everybody must eat some sweets—even diabetics are expected to enjoy a symbolic mouthful. These sweets are purchased from professional sweet makers but *patishapta* is a Bengali sweet that is made at home for this festival.

■ *Patishapta* ■
Serves 6/Makes 12-13 pieces

Filling:

Ingredients
1 cup desiccated coconut or ground flesh of $1/2$ fresh coconut
1 cup (250 g) brown sugar or jaggery/gur
(grated or finely chopped)

Method
Cook coconut and sugar over medium heat, stirring constantly until sugar has melted and slightly caramelized (10-12 minutes).
Allow to cool slightly.
Divide mixture into 12-13 portions and roll each into a 10-cm long log shape.

Crêpes:

Ingredients
1 cup semolina
1 cup plain flour (maida), shifted
1 tsp sugar

2 tbsp peanut oil or ghee
1 $\frac{1}{2}$ litres full cream milk
3 green cardamom pods

Method

Mix semolina, flour and sugar with ghee or oil.

Add enough milk to make a thin batter and mix thoroughly (you will need to beat out any lumps).

Heat a medium-sized frying pan and oil it very sparingly or alternatively use a non-stick pan.

Place a ladle full of batter into pan and cook until crêpe is golden.

On the edge of the crêpe place one of the coconut logs and then roll up the crêpe.

Turn and cook until brown all over.

To serve

Boil remaining milk with sugar to taste and a few cardamom pods until it reduces to a thick cream. Serve crêpes with cream liberally doused over them.

■ Diwali

If Holi is the most boisterous festival in Delhi then Diwali is the most beautiful. It is also the noisiest. Diwali marks the darkest night of the year and is celebrated in late October or early November. On this night the victorious Lord Ram returns home to Ayodhya with his wife Sita after fourteen years in exile. To light their way home, buildings, homes and offices are illuminated with rows of oil lamps, candles and fairy lights. The sky above the city is also lit up by thousands of fireworks displays, the sound of which can make Delhi a challenging place to be on Diwali eve.

Diwali is also the beginning of the Hindu financial year and, Lakshmi, the goddess of prosperity and wealth, is also worshipped. In the weeks prior to the festival, all Delhi stores have big sales. It is traditional to buy kitchenware and new clothing at this time and both are heavily discounted. Old debts and grievances are also meant to be settled or forgotten on Diwali and good fortune is to be wished to all. Gambling is a Diwali pastime; anyone who enjoys a winning streak during Diwali is supposed to enjoy good luck in the coming year.

It is traditional to give sweets on Diwali. Friends, relatives and business associates exchange boxes of *dry fruit* and *nuts* and *sweetmeats*. Most people prefer to buy Diwali sweetmeats from professional sweet makers (which typically have to be ordered some time in advance as Diwali is the busiest time of year for Delhi's confectioners), but some simple sweets can be made at home.

■ *Coconut Barfi* ■
Makes 25-30 pieces

Ingredients
2 cups desiccated coconut
1 cup coarsely shredded dry coconut
1 cup full cream milk
seeds of 1 green cardamom, crushed
$1^{1}/_{2}$ cups sugar
1 tbsp ghee

Method

Mix both coconuts together thoroughly in a heavy-based pan. Add milk and cook over medium heat until the mix comes to a gentle boil. Continue cooking for 10-12 minutes. Add cardamoms.

At the same time mix sugar with $^1/_2$ cup water and boil until soft thread stage is reached (a few drops of syrup dropped in iced water forms a soft 'thread' that clings together but can be stretched).

Gradually pour syrup into coconut mixture, stirring continuously.

Add ghee and continue stirring until a soft lump is formed.

Empty mix into a greased tin or container. Gently pat mixture smooth.

Allow to cool and cut into squares.

Store in an airtight container.

Since Diwali is spent devouring all the sweetmeats that have been received, to balance the act people like to have something savoury to nibble on.

■ Spicy Khaju ■
Makes 25-30 pieces

Ingredients
2 cups gram flour (besan)
$^1/_2$ cup plain flour (maida)
salt to taste
2 tsp red chilli powder (or to taste)
$^1/_2$ tsp ajwain
1 tsp cumin seeds
1 tbsp fresh coriander, finely chopped
ghee or oil to deep fry

Method

Sift both flours together with salt.

Make a well in the centre and add remaining ingredients except ghee or oil. Mix well.

Add enough cold water to make a soft dough. Knead lightly.

Roll out dough thinly. Cut out small rounds or strips and prick all over with a fork.

Allow to dry on a tea towel for 30 minutes.

Deep fry until golden in ghee or oil. Drain on kitchen paper.

Allow to cool and store in an airtight container.

■ Ramadan and Id-ul-Fitr

The ninth month of the Islamic lunar calendar is Ramadan. This is the month in which the Koran was revealed to the Prophet Mohammad. Ramadan is a month of fasting and it is incumbent on every Muslim over the age of twelve to not drink, eat, smoke, engage in sexual intercourse or think sinful thoughts between dawn to sundown for thirty days.

As the sun finally sets each evening during Ramadan, the area around Delhi's Jama Masjid comes alive with people making a beeline for hotels and cafes for *iftari* (breakfast). Here they enjoy steaming hot plates of *nehari* or *mutton cooked with wheat or dal*, and wash them down with plenty of *tea*. As it is a lunar festival, the dates for Ramadan change each year.

Ramadan ends with Id-ul-Fitr (Festival of Alms). On this day, after their baths, everyone wears new clothes that the women have worked on during Ramadan. On the

morning of Id-ul-Fitr, before attending the mosque for
prayers, a dish of *vermicelli cooked in milk with sugar, dry
fruit and nuts* is eaten (see recipe for Sheer khurma). Later
in the day, a huge feast is enjoyed at which the focus is on
meat dishes such as a *whole roasted sheep or goat*. The feast
always finishes with a rich sweet such as *shahi tukra*.

■ *Shahi Tukra (Fried bread sweet)* ■
Serves 6-8

Ingredients
1 tsp saffron strings
1 cup cream
$^{1}/_{4}$ cup almonds, sliced
$^{1}/_{3}$ cup pistachios, chopped
6 slices white bread
1 cup ghee
1 cup sugar
8 tbsp milk
2 tbsp sultanas or kishmish
2 tbsp rosewater
seeds of 5 green cardamoms, ground

Method
Put saffron in a bowl and pour over 2 tsp boiling water and 2
tbsp cream.

Dry-roast nuts in a frying pan or in an oven and set
aside.

Remove crusts from bread and cut each slice in half.

Heat ghee in a frying pan and fry bread, turning once till
golden on both sides. Keep aside.

Put 1 cup cold water and sugar in a pan and cook until

sugar dissolves. Cook uncovered on high heat for 5 minutes. Remove pan from heat and dip each piece of fried bread into syrup. Arrange bread slices in a shallow baking dish.

Pour milk and the rest of the cream into syrup and cook over medium heat for about 3 minutes, stirring constantly. Stir in soaked saffron and remove from heat.

Pour cream mixture over bread, sprinkle on nuts, sultanas, cardamom and rose water, and refrigerate. Serve chilled.

■ Christmas

Delhi's small Christian community is lucky enough to be able to enjoy Christmas without the encumbrance of the materialism it seems to generate in Christian countries. Delhi's shopkeepers don't let the chance go by to offer Christmas specials in the hope of encouraging consumers, but it is a relatively low-key sales campaign. The big hotels offer patrons traditional Christmas fare in the weeks leading up to Christmas and on the actual day. Hotel bakeries and European-style confectioners such as **Wengers** sells a range of Christmas goodies such as *mince pies, shortbread, Christmas pudding, brandy butter, gingerbread, marzipan*, and *bouche Noel* (French Christmas cake).

The British introduced the celebration of Christmas to Delhi long before there were hotel bakeries but they would have had little trouble procuring the dry fruit, nuts and spices they needed to make their traditional Christmas goods.

■ Sikh Festivals

Throughout the year the Sikh community of Delhi holds many festivals to celebrate the various anniversaries of their ten gurus. Everyday though, *langar* (communal meals) are offered at all **gurudwaras** in Delhi. Twenty-four hours a day, seven days a week, anyone, regardless of his or her religion, can arrive at the temple and be given a meal. The Sikhs believe that by eating together people create community and that the energy gained from food can then be put to benefit within the community.

The main gurudwara in Chandni Chowk houses a huge kitchen which is entirely staffed by volunteers. The meals offered at the gurudwara are simple but substantial: *roti*, *dal*, *curd* and *sabzi*. In another kitchen, the *prasad* that is offered each visitor on leaving the gurudwara is made.

■ *Prasad* ■
Serves 6

Ingredients
1 cup ghee
1 cup sugar
1 cup plain flour (maida)
1 cup hot water

Method
Melt ghee over medium heat. Add sugar and stir until dissolved. Add flour and cook until ghee is absorbed and flour is a golden colour. Add hot water and cook, stirring constantly until water is absorbed. Serve hot or cold.

Nine

■

STREET FOOD, SNACKS AND SWEETS

Delhi is famous for its street food. On nearly every street corner there will be someone selling some tasty, inexpensive eats. One could spend weeks sampling food from Delhi's **street vendors** and still be discovering new tastes. Delhiites patronize street vendors for both snacks and meals. Vendors situated in commercial areas do a brisk trade selling lunches and snacks to office workers.

Typically you will have to eat standing up (unless a wall or park bench is nearby) and use your fingers—unless the odd toothpick is provided. Your plate will be made of dried leaves held together with a couple of small sticks or folded from recycled paper and you will need to have your own napkin if you require one. What you will get though is some of the most delicious and inexpensive food in the city.

Due to the rudimentary nature of the typical street-side set-up and the subsequent lack of storage facilities, a street vendor only ever prepares enough food for one day. This may be prepared at home or on the street over a gas or charcoal fire but these circumstances dictate that the food will always be fresh.

Many of those who eat from street vendors may be forced to do so out of economic necessity but they can be as discerning about their choice of food as the man who can afford to eat in restaurants. If there is a crowd around a street vendor, it's worth stopping and sampling his wares. One of the most memorable dishes I have eaten in Delhi was a dish of robustly spiced *chana bhatura* served up from an old oil tin that was functioning as a cooking pot. I had chosen the vendor because he was doing a particularly brisk trade with the locals and I was not let down by 'local knowledge'.

The spectrum of food available on Delhi's streets ranges from simple slices of *fresh radish sprinkled with masala* to multi-faceted *chaat* that are created from several component items.

The arrival of summer in Delhi is heralded not only by rising temperatures and shorter tempers but also by the large number of *bhuttawallahs* who appear all over Delhi. The stock in trade for these street vendors are whole ears of succulent summer sweet corn roasted over makeshift charcoal braziers set up on carts or on the footpath itself. The roasted corn ears are served rubbed all over with lime juice and sprinkled with salt. For a few rupees it is one of the best snacks of a Delhi summer. The bhuttawallahs do not set up their business until early evening but temperatures still hover in the thirties and it must require quite some endurance to spend so many hours roasting ears of corn over the fire! As the summer winds up and the supply of sweet corn dwindles, the bhuttawallahs disappear.

In the late summer you will find street vendors in Old Delhi selling *freshly roasted water chestnuts*. The blackened skin may look uninviting but peel it away and the crisp nutty flesh inside is revealed. Other basic street snacks you can enjoy are fresh young *carrots peeled and sprinkled with spices and salt*, pieces of fresh, young *sugar cane* and boat-shaped slices of *fresh coconut*. (For those with sensitive stomachs or those not accustomed to India, it is prudent to not eat any food that has not been cooked. If you want to try these things, I suggest first peeling and washing them in clean water.)

Another simple snack you will find being sold on Delhi's streets is *namkeen* (a generic term for savouries). These are salty, spiced nibbles made up of varying combinations of *roasted or fried nuts*, *chickpeas*, *pulses* and *peas*. The more elaborate namkeen mixes will include crisp vermicelli noodles and crunchy savoury morsels. Both these additions are made from ground pulses that have been formed into a dough, shaped and fried (the smell of these being cooked is heavenly). A typical selection of basic namkeen would be *badam lachha* (roasted almonds), *kaju lachha* (roasted kaju), *mini samosas, moong ki dal, masala chips, potato straws, kabli chana, nut crackers, dal moth, aloo bhujia, moongphali*, and *spicy cornflakes*. These are sold separately or variously combined to create mixtures such as *sem beej panchphoran mix, meva mixture, navratan mixture* and so on.

The namkeen vendor sits on the pavement or on his cart surrounded by a display of his wares on large metal dishes or poking out of bulging bags. Alongside the namkeen he will have a set of scales and all day, people come past and purchase a weighed measure of namkeen to fill the hungry hours between meals.

Namkeen are not only sold by street vendors. You will find large displays of namkeen in many of Delhi's large sweet houses. Vendors and stores have their own unique mixes and people think nothing of driving to the other side of Delhi to buy their favourite (be warned: namkeen are addictive). Namkeen are inexpensive and know no class boundaries; they are eaten from a cone of recycled newspaper as often as they are nibbled from a crystal bowl in Delhi's most elegant homes. If you are having a drink in any of Delhi's hotels, you are likely to be presented with a bowl of some type of namkeen as accompaniment. Namkeen have even become a part of a social reform programme for the inmates of Delhi's Tihar jail.

In a remarkable show of social foresight, the jail has set up an innovative scheme whereby inmates can become involved in producing a range of namkeen. They are sold in Delhi stores under the brand name *TJ's*. Each packet carries the slogan 'help us keep the city crime free'. The inmates who work to produce the namkeen earn about Rs 600 a month, which they are able to send home to their families. Once they leave jail, those who were involved in the programme are able to continue their association with the product by selling it.

As moorish as namkeen are, they do not a meal make. So when you find yourself on the streets of Delhi looking for something a bit more substantial, what you should be looking for is chaat. Delhi is renowned for its chaat and while technically a snack, it can also pass as a light meal. A typical chaat will include something fried, some curd, a slick of chutney or spiced sauce and a sprinkling of chaat masala.

■ *Chaat Masala* ■

Ingredients
1 tsp freshly ground black pepper
1 tsp roasted ground cumin seeds
1 tsp ginger powder
1 tsp rock salt (lohri namak)
1 tsp black salt (kala namak)
1 tsp red chilli powder (or to taste)
1 tsp mango powder (amchur)
$1/2$ tsp asafoetida powder (hing)
1 tsp brown sugar (optional)

Method
Mix all ingredients together and store in an airtight jar.

Delhi chaat has a reputation for being well spiced with chilli and there is a historical explanation for this. During Shah Jahan's reign he directed Ali Mardan Khan to rebuild an old canal (that had been constructed during the reign of Jehangir) and redirect it to run down the centre of Chandni Chowk. The canal provided water for much of Delhi's population and it drew its supply from the Yamuna river a considerable distance upstream from Delhi. Half a century later, when the Mughal fortunes began to decline, the canal was in shambles. A renowned hakim (traditional Muslim doctor) announced that the water in the Chandni Chowk canal was full of ill humours. On the journey down from its clean source, the water in the canal was open to all including animals, and often served as a 'receptacle of every kind of filth'. To counter the effect of these water-borne ill humours, the esteemed hakim recommended adding a good amount of red chillies to food as he considered these to be efficacious in killing germs. Thus developed the Delhi taste for chilli and Delhi's street vendors have retained the habit of adding generous doses of chilli to their food.

Many chaatwallahs have a permanent location, so when you discover one you like, it's easy to revisit.

At **Lajpat Nagar Central Market** there is a street-side dye works where the ladies of Delhi go to have dupattas and pieces of cloth dyed. While this dyeing process is remarkably quick, it is by no means instant. To fill the time one can enjoy some of the chaat that this market is known for.

Directly opposite the dye works there is a chaatwallah selling *moong ki pakode*. From mid-morning until early evening he is kept busy scooping up handfuls of batter (made from ground moong dal that has been left to ferment overnight) and dropping it in perfect rounds into a huge cauldron of hot oil. The gas caught in the batter from the fermentation process causes the pakode to puff up when dropped in the oil and the result is a crisp, golden fritter with a tender inside. Served smothered with a coriander and *green chilli chutney* and a small mound of tangy *mooli salad*, this snack borders on the sublime.

Adjacent to the *moong ki pakode* stall there is a lone vendor with a veiled basin on a small bamboo tripod. From behind this veil he creates a refreshing chaat of cooked *month dal,* cubed boiled potato, chopped tomato, lemon juice, coriander and masala. He places all the ingredients in a leaf plate and then flicks his wrist and tosses it to mix it all up. A small plate of this chaat and one of moong ki pakode will fortify you for a round of bartering at the market.

Aloo tikki is a street snack that you will see being cooked up all over Delhi. On a large flat iron plate the chaatwallah fries these lightly spiced potato patties until they are golden and then serves them with a coriander or chilli chutney and a sweet-and-sour tamarind sauce. Next

Aloo tikki at Lajpat Nagar

to the moong ki pakode wallah in Lajpat Nagar there is a chaatwallah selling aloo tikki. In **GK I Market** there is a very popular (and very clean) chaatwallah (adjacent to Prince Paan) who serves up excellent aloo tikki to hungry shoppers. **Shree Prabhu Chaat** has been selling chaat for over fifty years and is a Delhi institution for aloo tikki and *golgappas* or *paani puris*. **Golooji Chaat-Waat** in the Eatopia complex at the Habitat Centre serves not only aloo tikki but a variation in *hare matar ki tikki*. These lightly spiced green pea patties come dressed with mint chutney, mango chutney, curd, *chaat masala* and a sprinkling of crunchy namkeen.

Another favourite in Delhi is golgappas. These light and crispy fried puffs (made of wheat or semolina) are broken open and a few small pieces of boiled potato and cooked chickpeas popped inside. The puff is then dipped in *jal zeera*—a spicy liquid of water mixed with mango, kachri (dried melon), ginger, chillies, cumin seeds, peppercorns and black salt. There is a bit of a skill involved in eating golgappas so that you don't choke on the liquid as you bite on the puff. Golgappa-eating competitions are a favourite sport amongst Delhi school boys.

Street vendors selling golgappas can be identified by the rectangular glass case filled with the empty pastry shells that sits atop their cart. These vendors usually also sell *papri chaat*. To make this chaat, a generous plateful of papris (flaky cumin-flavoured pastry discs) are dressed

A chaatwallah at Chandni Chowk

with curd, potato and chickpea mixture, a generous dollop of unctuous sweet-sour tamarind chutney, green chutney (coriander and green chillies), and the requisite sprinkle of chaat masala. Papri chaat is finger-licking delicious and it is interesting to note that the word 'chaat' means 'to lick'. Papri chaat is easy to prepare at home.

■ *Papri* ■
Serves 6

Ingredients
1 $^1/_2$ cups plain flour (maida)
$^1/_2$ tsp salt
1 tsp cumin seeds
2 tbsp ghee, melted
ghee for deep frying

Method

Sift flour and salt. Add cumin seeds and mix well. Add enough cold water to make a soft dough. Knead melted ghee into dough until soft.

Roll out thinly. Cut out small discs from the dough. Prick with a fork.

Deep fry discs in ghee until golden, Drain on kitchen paper.

(As an alternative I sometimes bake the discs on an oven tray that has been lightly greased with ghee—not traditional but lighter).

■ Sonth ki Chutney ■

Ingredients
$1/2$ cup tamarind pulp
$3/4$ cup jaggery (gur), chopped
1 tsp rock salt (lohri namak)
1 tsp black salt (kala namak)
1 tsp ginger
1 tsp roasted, ground cumin seeds
$1/4$ tsp black pepper powder
$1/4$ tsp red chilli powder

Method

Soak tamarind in 1 cup hot water until soft and pulpy.

Strain pulp and water through a sieve, pushing it through with the back of a wooden spoon to extract all the pulp.

Add remaining ingredients and bring to boil. Simmer over low heat until it thickens a little. Cool.

■ Hare Dhaniya ki Chutney ■

This chutney is very versatile and can be served with many of the dishes in this book: nargisi kofta, seekh kabab, pakoras, Jain croquettes etc.

Ingredients
1 bunch washed coriander leaves
1 tbsp peanuts, coarsely ground
$^1/_4$ cup chopped green chillies
2 tsp salt
1 tsp sugar or crushed jaggery (gur)
1 tbsp lime juice

Method
Grind coriander, peanuts and chillies to a fine paste.
Add salt, sugar and lime juice. Mix well and serve.

To assemble for Papri Chaat

Ingredients
papri
curd whipped smooth with a fork
chutneys
chaat masala

Method
Put papri on a plate, smother with curd, add a generous dollop
of both chutneys and a sprinkle of chaat masala.

In ancient Delhi the foods that were most enjoyed were
small fried cakes made of ground pulses or grains
'sprinkled' with curd and spiced sauces. It is interesting
to note that most of the chaat that you find in Delhi is
basically a variation on this. A good example of the
longevity of these ancient tastes is Delhi's most famous
chaat, *dahi bhalla chaat*. Ground white *urad dal* is made
up into small balls which are then fried in ghee or oil.
Before serving, the bhallas are soaked in warm water and
then squeezed to remove any excess water and oil. This

also gives the bhallas a unique soft texture. To serve, the bhallas are doused with curd and a well-spiced sweet mango chutney. You can enjoy this chaat from street vendors but Delhi's favourite place to eat it is **Natraj Dahi Bhalle Wala** in Chandni Chowk. If you fancy contemplating the busy street life then order some dahi bhallas from the simple narrow takeaway counter on the street or you can retire upstairs to the more secluded and spacious seating area. *Phal chaat* (fresh seasonal fruit cut into chunks and sprinkled with chaat masala) is another common street snack. **Chaatwallah** in Chandni Chowk is the best-known purveyor of this treat.

If you are eager to try these delicious snacks but feel concerned about eating food from street stalls then the best option is to visit one of Delhi's reputable 'sweet houses' where you can try them. **Bengali Sweet House** is the Delhi equivalent of a fast-food barn (except that the food here is much better). You can get all sorts of snacks and fast meals here, including Indianized Western-style fast foods, but most importantly, you can sample street snacks such as *golgappas*, *papri chaat* and *aloo tikki*. **Nathu's Sweet House** (several branches), **Haldiram's** (several branches) and **Sweets Corner** are also good places to visit for snacks. Opposite Sweets Corner under a shady tree, there is a chaatwallah selling tasty *bhel puri*. Technically this is a Mumbai street food but that doesn't stop Delhiites from enjoying it.

Sweets play an important role in Delhi life. Besides

satisfying the renowned Delhi sweet tooth, they are routinely offered to guests and are also a traditional gift at Diwali.

The Indian sweets that you will find in Delhi can be roughly categorized as dry sweets and wet sweets. The dry ones include *barfi*, *laddoos* and some *halwas*. Laddoos are made from besan, sugar and ghee and are commonly offered as *prasad* to the gods. Halwas can be made of wheat, nuts, carrots, ground pulses or pumpkin. The consistency of the halwa sold in sweet shops is a cross between a firm jelly and a fudge (a halwa with a much looser consistency is made at home as a dessert). Wet sweets include Bengali specialties such as *rasomalai* and *rasogolla*. A comprehensive listing of the varieties of sweets available in Delhi would be a book in itself and details of their preparation another one. So let us suffice here to give you a brief taste and direct you towards some of Delhi's venerated sweet sellers.

Tewari Brothers in Chandni Chowk is famous for its laddoo. There is usually a crowd milling about the front of this inconspicuous shop and getting inside to buy some ghee-rich laddoo often requires a bit of push and shove. Further up Chandni Chowk on the left side of the Fatehpuri Mosque gateway you will find **Bikaner Bhujia Bhandar**. Delhiites come here to buy their famous *Karachi halwa*. This firm, chewy, halwa is a bit tricky to make which is why people prefer to buy it, but here is a recipe if you feel you want to try.

■ *Karachi Halwa* ■
Makes 16 pieces

Ingredients
500 g castor sugar
115 g cornflour (from wheat not corn) or arrowroot
yellow food colouring
2 tsp lime juice
ghee as required
60 g almonds
30 g pistachio nuts

Method
Dissolve sugar in 3 cups water and boil for 5 minutes.

Strain through a seive lined with muslin.

Mix cornflour with $1^1/_2$ cups cold water to form a thin paste. Add food colour.

Cook, stirring constantly, over medium heat until mixture turns into a lump.

Add lime juice and keep stirring. Gradually add sugar syrup and stir. When mixture sticks to base of pan add 1 tbsp ghee. Repeat this step until mixture becomes one lump.

Mix in nuts.

Pour into a greased pan and smooth down with the back of a greased spoon.

Allow to cool and cut into squares or diamonds.

Haldiram's at Chandni Chowk is a veritable treasure chest of brightly coloured and decorated sweets. They also sell a range of snacks and savouries some of which are as brightly decorated as their sweets. I estimate that you could try something new in this store everyday for a year and still not have exhausted their variety. Haldiram's has also built up a considerable business selling a range of packaged namkeen to both the domestic and international markets.

The Delhiite's love of sweets extends past Indian varieties, and *European-style cakes* and *pastries* are popular and easily available. Many of Delhi's international hotels have pastry shops where patisserie can be purchased. These are all of a consistently high quality but do not expect to find them filled with fresh cream. The milk in India doesn't have the high fat content of the milk of Western cows and it is difficult to whip Indian cream into a firm stand-alone mass. (The heat and humidity don't help much either.) Consequently, most European-style cakes and pastries available in Delhi are filled and iced with a butter cream.

Wengers in Connuaght Place is the oldest European-style cake shop in the city. The refrigerated cabinets house a huge variety of cakes, pastries, biscuits and savouries. **Sugar and Spice** is a chain of stores that specializes in continental-style cakes, pastries and small goods. **Nathu's** in Bengali Market has a pastry shop that also stocks a large range of European-style biscuits.

No chapter on snacking in Delhi would be complete without mention of **Keventers** in Connaught Place. You can drop into this small cave-like shop for snacks such as *cheese pakoras* and *vegetable seekh kababs* but the real drawcard here are the *milkshakes*. These come in a wide variety of flavours in old-fashioned, pint-size milk bottles that make you feel like you're a child again!

SHREE PRABHU CHAT
(In front of the UPSC offices)
Shahjahan Road
8.00 a.m.-8.00 p.m.

GOLOOJI CHAAT-WAAT
Eatopia
Habitat World
Indian Habitat Centre
Lodhi Road
24682222

NATHU'S SWEETS
23, 24, 25 Bengali Market
23711731

NATHU'S SWEETS HOUSE
Community Centre
New Friends Colony
26921055
10 a.m.-11 p.m.

NATHU'S SWEETS &
PASTRY SHOP
2 Sunder Nagar Market
24354982
8.30 a.m.-10.30 p.m.

BENGALI SWEET HOUSE
27-37 Bengali Market
23711064, 23355591
8 a.m.-11 p.m.

SWEETS CORNER
1 Sunder Nagar Market
246119261

HALDIRAM'S
Chandni Chowk
(Near Gurudwara Seesganj)
22516343, 22925334

45 Ring Road
Lajpat Nagar
26830584

Mathura Road
Sarita Vihar
26959546

Delhi-Jaipur Highway
Gurgaon
0124-6372410

TEWARI BROTHERS
862 Chandni Chowk
23918326, 23927690
7 a.m.-9 p.m.

BIKANER BHUJIA BHANDAR
1446 Chandni Chowk
22911696
8 a.m.-9 p.m.

NATRAJ DAHI BHALLE WALA
1396 Chandni Chowk
22917228
11 a.m.-10 p.m.

KEVENTERS
(Corner of Connaught Place
and Radial Road No. 3)
9 a.m.-Midnight

WENGERS
A-16 Connaught Place
23324437
10.30 a.m.-8 p.m.

SUGAR AND SPICE
Stores at:
GK 1 M-block Market
Indian Oil Bhavan, Janpath
10 a.m.-8 p.m.
Khan Market
Vasant Vihar

Hotels with pastry shops
include:
Ashoka Hotel
Hyatt Regency
ITC Maurya Sheraton
Le Meridien
The Oberoi
The Park
The Surya Hotel

Ten

■

WHERE TO SHOP

Everyday the streets of Delhi's residential neighbourhoods are busy with vendors selling *fruit and vegetables* from their carts. Some push them up and down the street loudly hawking their wares, others choose a shady spot under a tree and wait for the passing trade, still others will ring doorbells and offer their goods directly to the lady of the house. Much of Delhi's daily food shopping is conducted with these vendors.

These street vendors can't meet all a household's food needs though and a shopping expedition is needed at least once a week to replenish provisions.

■ Fruit and Vegetables

Sarojini Nagar Market is best known for selling excess export clothing and house wares but there is also an excellent fruit and vegetable market there. There is an enormous variety of fresh produce available here and the quality is very good. There is a long row of vegetable stalls on one side of the market and half a dozen fruit stalls in front of the market. (Fruit and vegetables are rarely sold from the same stall in Delhi.)

There are several fresh fruit stalls at the front of **INA** (Indian National Army) **Market**. Baskets of fruit are always well-received gifts in Delhi and the fruitwallahs at INA can create visual masterpieces with a simple basket, a few apples and oranges, a melon and plenty of cellophane and ribbon. There are several fruit stalls at **Khan Market** that offer the best local produce along with a wide variety of top quality imported fruit and vegetables. The prices are high but if you must have Australian grapes or Californian peaches during the winter months, this is where you will find them. On **Josip Broz Tito Marg** near Krishi Vihar there are two roadside fruit stalls that sell good quality fruit.

■ Fruit

Lychee (Leechi)

When you spot the first lychees piled up in vibrant red-and-green bunches on roadside carts you know summer has come to Delhi. One of the great pleasures of the hot season is breaking open the rough red skin of a lychee and biting into the firm opalescent flesh and revelling in the sweet perfumed nectar that floods your mouth; the intensity of the fruit seems to match the intensity of the heat.

The lychees that are available in Delhi come from

Dehra Dun and Bihar. Lychees from Bihar have an elongated oval shape, the Dehra Dun variety is more rounded; both are magnificent.

Once lychees make an appearance, it is wise to enjoy them immediately as the lychee season is short (May to June) and the fruit disappears as quickly as it appears.

Mango (Aam)

Along with lychees, mangoes are the other great pleasure of a Delhi summer. Mangoes have been enjoyed in India for thousands of years and much myth and legend has built up around the fruit in Hindu and Buddhist literature. Both the mango fruit and the leaves are considered auspicious and the fruit is considered a symbol of everlasting love. The Mughals eagerly took to mangoes and spent much energy in grafting them to create new varieties. It was the Portuguese in Goa that first introduced grafting to India and they were instrumental in developing many of the 1100 varieties of mango that are grown in India. Varieties such as the Alphonso bear their Portuguese heritage in their name. The paisley motif that the English appropriated from India is actually a mango.

The mango season is eagerly anticipated throughout India. The first specimens to appear on fruit carts in early summer may not be the best mangoes, but the sight of them brings the anticipation to an almost unbearable edge.

Everybody has their favourite mango and there is often passionate argument over the merits of different varieties: juicy, stringy, sweet, tart, firm, perfumed. *Alphonso*, *safeda*, *peri*, *langra* and *dusseri* are the common and commercial varieties that are usually available in Delhi throughout the summer, though each comes into season at a different time. A good way to familiarize yourself with these and some of the less commercial mango varieties is to attend the mango fair that is held in Delhi every July (see the chapter 'Festivals').

Before living in Delhi I was under the impression that I had eaten good mangoes, but no mango I had ever eaten before could compare with the flavour and sweetness of the mangoes in Delhi. Huge piles of fresh mangoes would appear on the local fruit carts and mindful of their season, I determined to enjoy at least one everyday. People told me that I would get sick from eating too many mangoes or that I would get horrid white pimples around my mouth, but neither of these things happened. Eating lots of mangoes simply left with me glowing with good health— probably the result of all that beta carotene!

The mango season runs from April to July. Mangoes don't just disappear overnight like lychees. The supply begins to recede and they become harder and less juicy and then one day the mango sellers do not appear and there are no more mangoes until the next summer.

Custard Apples (Sitaphal)

As summer draws to a close, some compensation for the disappearance of mangoes arrives in the form of the custard apple. This knobbly green fruit starts appearing on fruit stalls around August and stays on until November. The rich, creamy flesh of the custard apple has a more subtle flavour than the highly perfumed mangoes and lychees, but the milder temperatures of summer's closing days do not demand such distractions.

The fruit sellers in Chittaranjan Park usually offer the best specimens as they are a favourite fruit of the Bengali community.

Guavas (Amrood)

Late summer also sees the appearance of huge piles of guavas at fruit stalls. Guavas are available from August to November. These rather plain-looking fruit fill the air with their distinctive perfume and vendors swat flies with bunches of aromatic guava leaves. There are both pink- and white-fleshed guavas although both look the same from the outside; the white-fleshed variety being the more common. Guavas are native to Peru and did not come to India until the sixteenth century.

Guavawallahs always have a supply of masala on hand to sprinkle on slices of fresh guava.

Apples (Seb)

Apples come into Delhi from the cooler hill regions of Himachal Pradesh and Kashmir and are extremely good when they are in season (October to May) but can be mealy and soft at other times of the year. *Golden Delicious* and *Red Delicious* are the local commercially grown varieties of apples. The fruit shops in Khan Market have imported apples available all year round. Look out for the *Gold Medallion* brand of apple juice made in Himachal Pradesh—it is very good.

Bananas (Kela)

India is home to over a dozen different bananas (and there are that many names again for them). You will see various bananas available throughout the year although *cavendish bananas*—both dwarf and regular varieties— are the most common.

Grapes (Angoor)

Grapes are in season from August to November and both green and red varieties appear at the market stalls.

Citrus Fruit

Nimbu are small Indian limes that are used as one would use lemons. Different varieties of lemons—grown in the hill regions—sometimes make an appearance at Delhi fruit stalls. The nimbu is indispensable in the Delhi kitchen and is available all year round.

Several varieties of oranges are available in Delhi: *kinu*, an orange and tangerine hybrid that has very few pips, *santhra*, a loose-skinned citrus similar to a mandarin, *mosambi*, a bright-green orange with pale flesh that is used for juicing and *malta*, a navel orange.

Sand Apples Sapodilla (Cheeku)

This fruit came to India from Latin America. Cheekus have a sweet, rich, meaty flesh and a sandy texture—hence the name sand apple. They are best eaten very ripe and are often used in milkshakes and ice-creams.

They are available in Delhi from November to March.

Papaya (Papita)

Another Latin American native, the papaya is available all year round in Delhi. It makes a good breakfast sliced up and served with cheeku.

Melons

There are different varieties of melons available all year round in Delhi and they have always been a popular fruit here. The small perfumed netted melons (*kharbooja*) have been grown and eaten in Delhi since the city's earliest days. Watermelon (*tarbooj*) comes from Rajasthan and is available from March to June. The Mughals introduced other varieties of melon to the city and the big oval yellow melons that you see around are from Afghanistan.

Mulberries (Shehthooth)

The Mughals introduced mulberries to Delhi and there are a large number of mulberry trees in the city. The trees bear fruit from May to June and it is a popular sport with young boys to climb the trees to pick the fruit. Mulberries look like elongated blackberries and there is also a white variety.

Pears (Naspati)

Towards the end of summer, tiny pears from Kashmir start appearing on fruit carts. They do not look inspiring but they are incredibly sweet and tender. Larger *William Pears* are also available.

Pomegranate (Anar)

This most ancient of fruits came to India from Iran 4000 years ago. Pomegranate juice is very popular in Delhi and the pips (*anardana*) are often used to garnish chaat. Pomegranates are available August to December.

Other fruit

Cherries, *apricots* (*khoobani*), *plums* and *peaches* (*arhoo*) are grown in the cooler hill districts and are available in

Delhi in May, June and July. *Strawberries* from the plains are available in Delhi in March and April.

■ Vegetables

There are a number of common vegetables that are available all year round in Delhi: creamy white *cauliflower* (phool gobi), *eggplant* or *brinjal* (baingan) *potatoes* (aloo), *onions* (piaz)—onions are always red or the Spanish variety—*carrots* (gajar), *green capsicum* (Shimla mirch), *tomatoes* (tamatar), *cabbage* (bandha gobi), *cucumber* (kheera)—these are often very dark, nearly black, with yellow patches—fresh *ginger* (adrak), *garlic* (lasun), *peas* (matar) and *spinach* (saag).

For those who are not Delhi residents, some of the vegetables that you may find unusual are:

Fenugreek leaves (Methi)

Bunches of fenugreek leaves are commonly cooked with potatoes. *Methi* is a winter vegetable and has small round leaves and imparts a tangy flavour. It is also called the 'spinach of the poor'.

Bitter Gourd (Karela)

The name of this vegetable is very apt as it is indeed bitter. You can apparently de-bitter them by salting prior to cooking but it has never worked for me! *Karela* is considered to have medicinal properties and is a popular vegetable in Delhi. I think a taste for karela is something that you have to be born with!

Okra (Bhindi)

Also known as *lady's fingers*, this vegetable is a member of the hibiscus family.

Colocasia (Arbi)

Also known as *taro*, this dark brown root vegetable is popularly eaten fried in thick slices in vegetarian households.

Radish (Mooli)

These long white radishes are cut up into pieces as a snack or grated as a salad. Pieces of radish are also eaten as a relish with meals.

Jackfruit (Kathal)

Another ancient Indian food, this large green fruit is actually cooked as a vegetable; it has a fleshy texture when cooked and is delicious when cooked in a curry.

Plantain (Kaccha kela)

These are large green bananas that are used for cooking and considered a vegetable.

Gourds

Gourds are native to India and are an ancient food. There is always a variety of gourd available in the market: *bottle gourd* (louki), *tinda*, a small round gourd that is well liked for its tenderness, *ash gourd* (petha), cooked as a vegetable or candied to make the confection called *petha* and *pormal* which looks like a smooth-skinned, pale cucumber.

Gourds are cooked in curries but you can cook them as you would any marrow or squash.

If you want to purchase vegetables and herbs such as broccoli, bokchoy, iceberg lettuce, celery, leeks, bean shoots, dill or basil, there are several vegetable stalls at **INA Market** that specialize in *European and Asian vegetables*. The prices here are fairly high but the quality is good.

■ Fish

Delhi's fishmongers can look like a terrifying bunch perched as they are behind huge upright scimitar-like blades. This blade serves every need the fishmonger has—he uses it to scale the fish, he slides the fish gently down the blade to open its belly and remove the guts, he then passes the blade between flesh and bone to come up with clean fillets; he will even cut this up into smaller pieces if you request.

Bengalis are well known for their love of fish and seafood, so it is fitting that the Bengali-dominated suburb of **Chittaranjan Park** should have an excellent fish market. Around Durga Puja time (see chapter 'Festivals'), this market is brimming with varieties of fish.

Fish at Chittaranjan Park Market No. I

If you are buying fish from this market, be aware that Bengalis prefer fish with bones. They have a marvellous ability to separate the bones from the fish flesh with their tongues and then keep a little ball of the bones to one side in their mouth. If you do not possess this talent, you might like to ask for a relatively boneless variety.

At the back of INA Market there are five stalls selling a large variety of fish and in **Yusuf Sarai** you will find **Gujarat Fisheries** and **National Fisheries of India**. These two shops are adjacent to each other and both sell good quality fish. What is available changes seasonally and on a daily basis. There is a board that lists what is available on that day. The fishmongers here will cheerfully clean and fillet the fish to your requirements.

The fish that is sold in Delhi comes into the city from all over the country. Some common fish available in Delhi are:

Bekti (Bhetki)

A big fish with firm flesh that is also referrd to as 'salmon' in some shops, it is a type of sea perch.

Pomfret

Pomfrets come to Delhi from around Mumbai. A small dinner plate-shaped fish with mild flesh that is usually cooked whole.

Mackerel (Surmai)

A long round fish without scales that has a firm mild flesh.

Morrul

Very like sole.

Rohu

A river fish with lots of bones and soft flesh.

Hilsa

An estuary fish that is very popular with Bengalis. The flesh is tender and flavourful but it has lots of very small fine bones.

Prawns (Jhinga)

Very popular in Delhi, *burra jhinga,* large or jumbo prawns are also available.

Fresh live crabs (*kenkra*) and eels can also be bought from the Bengali fish market in Market No. I, Chittaranjan Park.

Bombay Duck

This is not a duck at all but a pungent, dried salted fish that is added crumbled to food for its distinctive flavour. In the main stall of **INA Market** there is an old woman

sitting up on a cart who sells Bombay Duck and other
dried fish.

■ Meat

Meat in Delhi means *mutton* (goat) or *buffalo*. If you want
to buy buffalo there are several butchers in **Nizamuddin**
who sell it—you can tell it is buffalo as the fat is white
(beef fat is yellow). Carcasses are strung up and displayed
here so you can see what you are getting. These butchers
also sell mutton. *Gosht* is the Hindi word for meat and is
generally applied to mutton.

On the south side of the **Jama Masjid** in Old Delhi,
there are several butchers who sell mutton. You buy familiar
cuts of meat here as well as goats' heads and goats' trotters,
both of which are kept piled up in baskets at the front of
the stalls. A few live goats are kept tethered up at the
front of these butchers' shops, seemingly oblivious to their
impending fate.

Butchers in Delhi are usually Muslims and they are
very accommodating with boning out meat and making
mince (*keema*). Mutton can also be bought from shops
selling chicken. There is a butcher in the main lane of
INA Market (towards the back).

At the rear of **Khan Market** there are three butcher
shops that supply fresh meat and chicken. The meat is cut
to order in front of you.

■ Poultry

Chicken is the most common and easily available meat in Delhi and there are chicken shops in most neighbourhoods. These shops offer all the different cuts of chicken and a range of pre-prepared *chicken products*. Competition is tough in Delhi's chicken market and you will find that chicken shops will deliver even the smallest order to your doorstep.

There is an organization in Delhi called **MESH** (Maximizing Employment to Serve the Handicapped) and one of their projects is raising free-range chickens. These chickens are of very good quality and are larger in size than most other poultry that you find in Delhi. MESH chickens are also a little more expensive but worth it. You can visit the MESH office or you can arrange to have the chickens (minimum of two) delivered on a Friday.

Fresh chicken and ducks are available at **INA Market**— indeed they are so fresh they are still walking around. Choose your specimen and it will be dressed quickly for you (do not watch if you are squeamish).

Poultry anywhere in India never comes with the skin left on. The whole lot is ripped off to remove the feathers. If you want the skin left on, you can ask, but the results will be mixed—you may have to spend a lot of time with a pair of tweezers removing the root end of the feathers that are still embedded in the skin. It might just be easier to avoid any recipes that require the chicken to have its skin on. Indians prefer to eat roosters (*murgha*) and keep the chickens (*murghi*) for producing eggs.

Adjacent to the fish market in **Old Delhi**, there is a live poultry market. There are hundreds of birds piled up in cages here waiting to be sold; the smell is quite strong and these birds are intended for people who will butcher them themselves. You can sometimes buy *geese* and *ducks* here.

You can buy ducks, *capons*, *guinea fowls*, *quails* and *turkeys* from **The French Farm**.

■ Pork

Pigpo specializes in pork products including fresh meat, pork sausages and small goods. **Sugar and Spice** stores also keep a small range of small goods such as *bacon* and *salami*.

■ Dairy Products

Milk (Doodh) and Curd/Yogurt (Dahi)

Most Delhiites buy their milk from the numerous **Mother Dairy** booths around the city. I have affectionately dubbed these booths the 'electronic cow'. Milk is purchased by paying at the counter for a specified amount and then taking your stainless steel milk pail over to the designated dispensing machine. You place your pail on the tiled recess, push the button and the milk flows out into your container. It's quite ingenious—no paper or plastic container needed! Milk is also available in plastic pouches but the 'electronic cow' always seem to be most in demand—queues always form to use her stainless steel udders in the early morning and again around dusk.

Delhiites like to buy fresh milk everyday and what is left over from the previous day is turned into curd. It is only recently that packaged commercial curd has become easily available. Mother Dairy now sells their own brand and **Amul** and **Nestlé** brands of curd are also available in local stores. You can buy fresh curd from confectioners. If you want a regular supply, it's best to make your own.

To make curd

Bring one litre milk to boil, turn heat off as soon as milk starts to froth and rise. Allow milk to cool until it is luke warm. While milk is cooling take two tbsp of prepared curd and beat with a fork until smooth. Add to milk. Cover and set aside overnight. If the weather is cold you may need to wrap a blanket around the bowl. The temperate needs to be at least 30°C for the curd to set. If you like firm curd you may need to hang it in clean dry cloth or muslin to drain off some of the excess whey.

Paneer

Paneer is Indian cottage cheese and is made by boiling milk, adding some type of acid such as lemon juice, vinegar or dried melon (kachri). This acid splits the milk into solids and whey. The solids are then pressed together to create a firm cheese. Paneer is also typically made at home but it is available at Mother Dairy and in sweetshops.

There is a stall in INA Market (to the right of the main lane) that sells very good fresh paneer and fresh cream. It is hard to find fresh cream in Delhi (one usually has to be satisfied with UHT cream). You won't be able to whip this cream as it doesn't have enough milk fat in it, but it is still a lovely cream for making sauces or for pouring. Janatapriya Dairy is another source of good fresh cream.

Cheese

Cheese is not a common product in India. The climate of Delhi (and most of India) is certainly not conducive to producing the type of hardened, matured cheese of European countries. Modern Delhiites are starting to develop a taste for cheese though and the stores where cheeses are available are growing in number. Imported cheeses are expensive in Delhi but there is a growing range of Indian-made cheeses being produced (a lot of them made in Sikkim). A good yak cheese from Nepal is also available. **Steakhouse**, **Sugar and Spice** and **Sharda Store** all stock a good selection of local and imported cheeses.

■ Spices, Dry Fruit and Nuts

You can find spices, dry fruit and nuts and dried lentils, beans and pulses very easily in Delhi. These are all common items and neighbourhood markets will stock a selection of them. A good place to buy them is at the western end of Chandni Chowk next to the Fatehpuri Mosque in **Khari Baoli**. This bustling, jostling market has been operating since Old Delhi was called Shahjahanabad. No matter what time of day you come, the footpaths are busy and the road seems to continually be gridlocked with cycle rickshaws and overburdened porters loading or unloading from the back of cycle carts. Around Diwali time it can become almost impossible to negotiate the footpath, as additional stalls are set up on the streets to allow merchants to do a roaring trade in dry fruit and nuts.

The quality is good here and the prices competitive. You can purchase any amount you like—small or large— but you have to buy very large quantities to be given a wholesale price (nothing less than 50 kg). Everything is on display and the stall holders are quite willing for you to try before you buy.

■ Dry Fruit and Nuts

Nuts
almond—*badam*
cashew—*kaju*
peanuts—*moongphali*
pistachio—*pista*
chironji—an indigenous dark, red-skinned, elongated nut
            similar to a pine nut in texture
walnuts—*akhrot*

There are also a variety of seeds available that are eaten as a snack or used for cooking: *melon seeds* (chormagaz), *lotus seed* (makhane), *pumpkin seeds* (kaddu ke beej) and *watermelon seeds* (tarbooz ke beej). *White poppy seeds* (khus khus) are used as a spice.

You can buy shelled or unshelled nuts and nuts that have been salted and spiced. *Dried Kashmiri morels* may also be available, though you will have to ask for these as they are quite expensive and not usually on display.

Dry fruits

raisins/sultanas—*kishmish*

dates—*khajur*

figs—*anjeer*

apricots—*khoobani*—you may find yourself looking at something that looks like a wizened peach kernel if you ask for apricots. Don't be put off as these are from Kashmir and they are very sweet and lack the acidity of other dried apricots. Dried apricots also come in sheets.

mango—*aam*—dried mango pulp (*aam papad*), both sweet and savoury, come in sheets and are available in cellophane-tight packets

coconut—*nariyal*

Spices

Alongside the fruit and nut stalls in **Khari Baoli** there are many stalls selling spices. The ground spices are formed into colourful pyramids in stainless steel bowls or at the top of sacks. Many of the stalls have exactly the same items but it pays to check quality and prices amongst a few before committing to any serious purchase.

Spices

Cumin—*zeera*
Black mustard seeds—*rai*
Coriander seeds—*sabut dhania*
Cloves—*laung*
Ginger dried—*sonth*
Nutmeg—*jaiphal*
Onion seeds—*kalaunji*
Black pepper—*kali mirch*
Red chillies, whole—*sabut lal mirch*
Red chillies, powdered—*pisi hui lal mirch*
Rock salt—*lahori namak*
Black salt—*kala namak*
Saffron—*kesar*
Cardamom—*elaichi*
Cinnamon—*dalchini*
Mace—*javatri*
Mango powder—*aamchur*
Turmeric—*haldi*
Asafoetida—*hing*

There are several elderly Tibetan men and women squatting on the footpath in **Khari Baoli** with a small set of scales and a small pile of reddish brown lumps before them. They are selling hing or asafoetida. Hing is a resinous extract that is commonly used in Hindu and Jain cooking often to replicate the taste of garlic and onion when neither is used; it comes from Afghanistan.

Raw hing has an awful smell (not for nothing is it known by the names 'fetid gum' or 'devil's foot') but it is transformed in cooking and adds a distinctive but pleasant taste. You are unlikely to see the pure asafoetida sold here anywhere else, as it is typically sold as a powder that has been diluted with flour (it is an expensive spice).

If you keep walking past the spice stalls you will come to a number of shops selling *pickles and chutneys*. In between these pickle shops there is laneway called **Gali Batasha**. This street traditionally sells sugar and you will see sugar merchants with many different grades of sugar displayed in large flat stainless steel pans. You will notice some 'stalactite' forms there. These are called *misri chini* (sugar candy). In keeping with its sweet theme, the lane also houses a good many shops selling *sweet biscuits* and *jams and preserved fruits*.

The silver leaf (*chandi ki varak*) used to decorate sweets is also sold in this lane. Silver leaf is tasteless, odourless, and purely decorative and it won't grate on your fillings. It is made by beating a tiny piece of silver between two pieces of leather until it is gossamer thin.

If you don't want to make the trip to Old Delhi then

you can buy dry fruits, nuts and spices at **INA Market**. There is facility at INA to have your spices freshly ground. **Roopak Stores** in Karol Bagh has an excellent range of dry fruits, spices, spice mixes, namkeen, pickles and chutneys.

■ Groceries

Nearly every residential block in Delhi has a neighbourhood store or market that sells a range of everyday goods such as flour, sugar, processed packaged cheese, pasta, noodles, snack foods, sliced bread, toiletries, cleaning products, tea, coffee, soft drinks, canned foods etc. There is often an incredible variety of goods to be found in one small store and the shop assistant may have to climb a ladder to get the item you want (as the item you want may be tucked away in a corner where you can't spot it). Retail rental is very expensive in Delhi so not one centimetre of it is wasted. These neighbourhood stores are a hive of activity including all the neighbourhood gossip. If you need a plumber or taxi service or a cleaning lady you can often do no better than to ask the storekeepers for help—he will know exactly what is happening in the neighbourhood and who is looking for work. These small stores will generally deliver free of charge—even if it just one tube of toothpaste.

There are several shops at **INA Market** and **Khan Market** that stock a large range of imported groceries. If you are craving Vegemite, good imported chocolate (Indian chocolate is very sweet and waxy), American mayonnaise, or canned blueberries, you can get them here.

Neighbourhood markets may also have their own mill where you can buy freshly ground flour. **Bharat Flour Mill** in Kailash Colony Market sells freshly ground wheat, barley, corn and millet flours; you can even take your own grain and have it ground there.

■ Tea, coffee, wine and spirits

If you want to make good coffee then the best place to purchase either beans or freshly ground coffee is at **The South Indian Coffee Shop** in **Khanna Market**. The beans are the *robusta* variety from South India and are roasted and ground on the premises. They also sell coffee plungers and percolators as well of a range of *tea*. Packaged imported coffee is available at INA or any of the other shops selling imported groceries.

Tea is easily available in Delhi. Every corner store sells everyday tea. If you are interested in purchasing or sampling a wider range of high quality Indian teas, there are several excellent tea shops that you can visit. The friendly and knowledgeable family who run **Regalia Tea House** will happily spend time with you explaining the tea-making process and explaining all the different varieties they stock. You can sample any of the teas. They also stock organic tea and a very good herbal tea. **Mittal Stores** next door to Regalia is also good. In Old Delhi you can sample and buy tea at **Aap ki Pasand**.

If you find yourself feeling slightly criminal when you buy liquor in Delhi it's not surprising. The shops selling liquor are reminiscent of prison cells with their barred fronts and drab concrete walls and exterior. Stores selling alcohol are called 'English Wine Shops'. You won't find these shops full of wine but they are well stocked with Indian *beer, whisky, brandy, rum* and *gin*. Alongside these regulars you may find *vodka, sherry* and *port*—and a small selection of wine. There are several Indian brands of wine: *Grovers, Riviera, Bosca* and *Golconda*, but no local ones. If the store you are patronizing is in an area with a population of expats, they may stock some French or Italian table wines.

Liquor shops are not open on the first and seventh days of each month. (These days being pay days there is an attempt to try and prevent men hitting the liquor shops with their pay packets in hand.) The liquor stores are also closed on national holidays (dry days). Stores do not open until after 1.00 p.m. and stay open until 7.00 p.m. The limited trading hours are meant to act as a deterrent to drinking. While these measures are well meant, what happens is that on the evening before dry days and by 1.00 p.m. each afternoon, queues have formed in front of the counters and there is frantic pushing and shoving.

■ Kitchenware

There are good kitchenware shops at **INA Market** and **Khan Market**.

It's not easy to buy good quality kitchen knives in Delhi but if you want to get your current knives sharpened look out for the knife sharpener as he pedals around on his bicycle. This same bicycle becomes his work tool as he uses the pedals to turn the sharpening wheel attached to the front of his bike above the handlebars.

Fruit & Vegetables

SAROJINI NAGAR MARKET
IV Cross Road Sarojini Nagar
Closed Monday

INA MARKET
Aurobindo Marg
Closed Tuesday

BOMBAY FRUIT MART
54-A Khan Market
24617729, 24655865
8 a.m.-8.30 p.m.

ALLIED FRUIT AND FLORIST
Shop 58-B Khan Market
24619579, 24622509
8 a.m.-9 p.m.

Fish & Seafood

GUJARAT FISHERIES
3 Yusuf Sarai Community Centre
10 a.m.-7 p.m.
Closed Tuesdays

NATIONAL FISHERIES
4 Yusuf Sarai Community Centre
10 a.m.-7 p.m.
Closed Tuesday

Meat & Chicken

THE MEAT SHOP
9 Khan Market
24616558

SM Fresh Meat &
Chicken
71-A Khan Maket
24634889

Mirajuddin & Sons
Shop 17 Khan Market
24649821, 24619822

MESH
Nataraj Emporium,
(Off Aurobindo Marg)
near Hauz Khas

The French Farm
Mr Roger Langbour
M7/15 DLF Qutab Enclave
Phase II, Gurgaon
951246359701

Pigpo
9 Jor Bagh Market
24611723, 24626930
Closed Monday

Sugar and Spice stores
(See p. 237)

Dairy
Mother Dairy
Booths all over Delhi
(look for the trademark blue
'drop')

Janatapriya Dairy
Lajpat Nagar Central Market

'Alankar Road' Road
(Opposite the new picture
hall 3Cs)

Steakhouse
13/8 Jor Bagh Market
24611008, 24611129
Closed Monday

Sharda Store
71-B Khan Market
Rabindra Nagar
24693519

Spices & Dry Fruit
Roopak Stores
Ajmal Khan Road
Karol Bagh
25722569

Bharat Flour Mill
Kailash Colony Market
26413833

Tea & Coffee
The South Indian
Coffee Shop
Khanna Market
(Near Jor Bagh)

Regalia Tea House
12 Sunder Nagar Market
4350115, 4351007

MITTAL TEA HOUSE
12 Sunder Nagar Market
4358588, 4350667

AAP KI PASAND
15 Netaji Subhash Marg
Daryaganj
Delhi 110002

Liquor

Most areas in Delhi have an 'English Wine Shop'.
You are sure to find one in:

East of Kailash (Mount
    Kailash DDA CSC)
GK II (Masjid Moth)
Green Park
Hauz Khas Market
Khan Market

■

Eleven

DELHI: the modern city

Twenty-first century Delhi is a city where tradition and modernity live side by side and each goes about its business often with nary a glance at the other. In the lanes of Old Delhi, traditional Muslim women, clad in their enveloping black burkhas, do their daily shopping. The family home is the focus of their life and meals are prepared and eaten at home. Notwithstanding a few modern additions—a television and a refrigerator—their lifestyle has altered little from that of their grandmothers. Some kilometres away from Old Delhi are the bright new showrooms and boutiques of **Ansal Plaza** and **South Extension**. These temples to conspicuous consumption are the stamping grounds of Delhi's growing number of upwardly mobile working women; the lives of these Delhi women are markedly different from that of their grandmothers.

As Delhi's modern women take to the workforce, many liberate themselves from the family kitchen and waiting there for them with open arms are thousands of restauranteurs and caterers eager and ready to provide meals. Delhi has seen a boom in eating outside the home in the last ten years. Much of it is driven by the changes women have made to their lives. Every month in Delhi, several eating places open their doors for business and the pages of local magazines and newspapers are hard-pressed to keep up with listings and reviews for these new establishments.

Eating out has also become a modern social 'sport' in Delhi; friends vie with each other to be the first to try a recommended restaurant, or to reach the pinnacle of the sport by independently 'discovering' a new place. There is much social cache to be had by eating at and, most importantly, being seen at a 'hot' new eating spot. Affluent Delhiites are not shy about their money and eating out offers an opportunity to show off clothing, jewellery, and children. The dining rooms of the fashionable abound with women wearing exquisite silk saris, smartly tailored salwar-kameezes or the latest modern fashions accessorized with plenty of jewellery. The emphasis is very much on outward appearances; there is a lot of 'air kissing' and a style of backbiting that matches Indian food for its spicyness. All this makes for an interesting and lively modern restaurant scene in Delhi.

■ European Cuisine in Modern Delhi

Until recently there was truly little to be recommended in terms of continental or European food in Delhi. Most of it was ordinary to awful and all of it was overpriced. (Still vivid in my mind are the peas and carrots in a thick white sauce that I was served as part of an 'Italian' antipasto platter—it was more English boarding school than sunny Italy. Or the impressively named 'chicken gateau' that turned out to be a chicken sandwich drowned in mayonnaise that cost three times what a similar sandwich would have cost in any European city.) Delhiites are on the whole adventurous eaters and they are to be commended for that. They are always searching for fresh tastes and new styles of food. Perhaps their persistence in supporting the restaurants serving these 'continental' abominations has paid off because the European food offered in Delhi has improved dramatically.

The very modern **Diva** serves excellent, authentic Italian food. The pasta dishes are cooked 'al dente' and there is not a hint of spice or chilli to be detected (unless the dish calls for it). *Porcini gnocchi* are small wheat and potato dumplings in a masterly porcini sauce (the flavours in the sauce were perfectly integrated; there was no 'hole' in it). The *mezzaluna al taleggi* (cheese-stuffed ravioli) is light, slippery, and satisfying. The desserts receive the same attention as the main dishes and the *strawberry cheesecake* and the *pannacotta* are both delicious. Diva attracts an interesting mix of people which gives the place an appealing buzz.

The Italian-style Sunday brunch buffet at **La Piazza**

is always busy and draws a crowd of both Delhi's socially prominent and socially aspirant families. The colourful antipasto-style *buffet* includes paper-thin *cold cuts*, *Italian cheeses*, grilled and marinated *vegetables*, *salads* and a selection of *breads*. For dessert it's hard to resist the creamy layers of chocolate, marscapone and sponge biscuits that make up the traditional *tiramisu*. **San Gimignano** has wonderful Italian food; the courtyard setting is divine and it borders on obscenely expensive.

The Big Chill serves up a mixed menu of contemporary dishes. The *Algerian chicken platter* is a huge plateful of tender, garlicy, lemony roast chicken, grilled vegetables and salad. It's almost enough for two people and it's already earned itself quite a reputation! The *Lebanese platter* is made up of *babe guanos* (eggplant dip), *hummus* (chickpea dip), and *fatuous* (salad). The flavours of the platter are authentic but the miserly serving of bread is not (no Lebanese kitchen would ever serve a platter of dips with two small pieces of bread—and then charge for extra bread). There is a wide selection of *soups*, *pasta*, *pizza* and interesting *bakes* on the menu. This is not haute cuisine but it is good, modern, café food served in upbeat, bright surroundings by cheerful, obliging staff.

Fab Café is another bright young thing serving contemporary café food. The food here is wholesome and earthy with a distinct 'wholefoods' bent. Try a '*Fabwich*', a home-made wholemeal roll wrapped around a variety of fillings (grilled vegetables, hummus, lettuce, tomato chutney, grilled chicken, cheese etc), the *broccoli soup* (brimming with vitamins and vitality), the *chicken cacciatore* or a *brown rice salad*. You can finish off with a slice of *lemon cheesecake* or *apple tart with fresh cream*. Fab Café serves good *coffee* and you can be *tres* modern here and call in anytime to just 'do' coffee and cake. Check out the display of *wholegrain products* and *low-fat baked snacks* at the back of the café.

Perhaps the most interesting new arrival on Delhi's restaurant scene is the **Kasbah** complex in Greater Kailash I. Comprising a coffee shop, **Tazzo**, an Italian restaurant, **Spago**, an eastern European-inspired bar, **Bohemia** and a rooftop Indian restaurant, **Zaffran**, this is a place that will set new standards in Delhi. The variety of offerings show that the owners intend to please all tastes but rather than mixing up everything on one menu, they have wisely chosen to keep each style separate and authentic. The food served at Spago is full of the fresh ingredients and clean flavours that the cuisine of Italy is renowned for. Dishes such as *tomato bruschetta; sole with lemon butter; parsley and white wine sauce; grilled vegetable salad; pannacotta* and *ricotta tart* are all exemplars of Italian style. Great attention has also been paid to the interior design and fittings at Kasbah and the result is a stylish yet comfortable complex that would be an asset to any city anywhere in the world.

■ Fast Food

The market potential in populous cities with expanding middle classes such as Delhi is enormous and the global fast-food giants are eager to grab a large share of it. While the big names in fast food have been making inroads into Delhi (and India), the progress of their culinary cultural imperialism has been much slower here than is their usual track record. The world's most recognizable purveyor of fast foods does have a presence in Delhi but the number of stores operating is nowhere near what they had planned in relation to the number of people living in the city. But so determined are they to gain a foothold in India that they have allowed radical changes to be made to their standard format menu. Obviously beef 'hamburgers' are not served and there is a large number of vegetarian choices that do not appear on their menus anywhere else in the world.

Marketing gurus may not have achieved the results they had hoped for in encouraging Delhiites to adopt burgers and fries as a regular food, but they have been far more successful with pizza. Demand for pizza is high in Delhi and there are pizza joints springing up all over the city. It seems that the advertising campaigns of the international pizza chains present in Delhi have driven this demand but it is the locals who are serving up the best pizzas. **Pizza Pizza Express (San Marzano)** in Ansal Plaza offers good pizza—light, crisp crust, fresh fillings, restrained but sufficient amounts of cheese—and respite from hot weather. As the name suggests **Flavours of Italy** specializes in Italian food and there are a variety of authentic pizzas on their menu. When weather permits, there is a pleasant outdoor seating area here. Flavours of Italy also serves a commendable (American style!) *chocolate brownie*.

Why bother with imported fast food though, when Delhi has its own on offer? *Kathi rolls*—kababs wrapped in tissue-thin roomali roti, with coriander chutney and plenty of onions (optional)—are more delicious than any mass-produced hamburger could ever hope to be. Delhi's best kathi rolls can be found at the two ends of the dining-out scale. **Nizam's Kathi Kababs** are the patriarchs of kathis in Delhi. This straightforward place serves a large range of kathis (chicken, mutton, egg, paneer, mushroom, keema, and various combinations of these). If you prefer a more refined environment and some table service with your kathi kabab then visit **The Great Kabab Factory** at the Radisson Hotel or **Karim's** at Nizamuddin or Jama Masjid.

Tandoori food can be served as a sumptuous repast or it can be a quick and easy meal when a skewer full of tandoori cooked chicken, meat, or paneer is served wrapped in a fresh tandoori naan or roti. **Colonel's Kababz** is a Delhi institution that specializes in 'fast' tandoori meals. It is a stand-up-only place, but while you are waiting for your food you can pass the time watching the chefs at work deftly shaping dough into breads and threading iron skewers with various meats and vegetables. If you are not interested in taking the culinary entertainment you can sit in your car and the waiters will serve you there. For the times when you feel like making no effort at all, Colonel's Kababz also runs a very busy home-delivery service.

Paranthas have been a Delhi 'fast food' for over one hundred years and Paranthe wale Gali in Old Delhi is the traditional place to eat them. But if you don't feel like making the trip you could visit **Triveni Café** at the Mandi House Arts and Cultural centre. This busy café serves the students and patrons of this lively arts centre and the stuffed paranthas served here are reputed to be amongst Delhi's best. There is a very pleasant outdoor terrace where you can enjoy your paranthas accompanied by a cup of *chai* at your leisure. While you are here you can visit the numerous galleries or take in a cultural show.

There must be some nexus between students and paranthas because the **Ganga Dhaba** at Jawaharlal Nehru University also serves reputable ones. This is an open-air dhaba so it is best visited on a pleasant winter day or on a balmy late-summer night. The dhaba also lies directly under the airport flight path so you can entertain yourself by watching the planes as they fly closely overhead.

For a spectacular panoramic view of modern Delhi over your lunch or dinner go to **Parikrama**, Delhi's very own revolving restaurant. It takes ninety minutes for the restaurant to complete a full revolution, so eat slowly. The food is a mixed menu of Indian, Chinese and Continental (the food is not the drawcard here but it's not bad and it's a fun place to eat).

■ Ice-cream

It is not surprising that a city that spends much of the year enduring sweltering temperatures has a love affair with ice-cream. The indigenous **Nirula's** chain has twenty-one branches that serve a constantly evolving range of twenty-one flavours. Their ice-cream is excellent but the best treat of all is a Nirula's *hot chocolate fudge sundae*. In the humble opinion of this writer, it is the very best chocolate ice-cream sundae in the world (and there are plenty like me who share this opinion). **Gourmet Ices** serves the sort of luscious ice-cream that people will drive across town for (and given that driving across Delhi is no mean feat, that says something). On my habitual visits to this subterranean ice-cream parlour, I methodically sampled (almost) all the ice-creams available there. My verdict is that *roasted fig and almond*, *mango*, and *coconut* are the best flavours.

The long green lawns of **Rajpath** beckon people to lounge about on them on Delhi's long hot summer nights and once you have found yourself a spot on the grass, you don't have to move very far to purchase an ice-cream. Ice-cream vendors selling a variety of local brands—

Kwality, Amul, Mother Dairy—pack the Rajpath kerb and the long rows of illuminated carts are quite picturesque in the night.

The Big Chill has a good reputation for their home-made ice-creams and the decadent desserts that accompany them. Signature ice-cream flavours such as *Kit Kat, chocolate Oreo* and *maple walnut chocolate chip*, paired with sinful desserts like *Banoffee pie, Mississippi mud pie, superfudge brownies*, and *chocolate truffle cake* are drawing in the crowds.

During the summer months, Delhi's large hotels have ice-cream festivals where they offer all manner of sundaes, ice-cream desserts, thick shakes, *sorbets* and traditional iced milk drinks such as *thandai* and *panna*.

■ Drinking in Delhi

Delhi cannot be described as a liberal city when it comes to liquor. Delhi's liquor laws are prohibitive and if you want to just go out and have a drink in Delhi, you are pretty much restricted to the bars of five-star hotels or private clubs (if you know a member). A number of 'pubs' and 'bars' have recently opened in Delhi but these are actually restaurants that serve drinks with food.

You certainly have to pay for the pleasure of drinking at five-star hotels but the surroundings are usually very pleasant. The **Patiala Peg** in The Imperial has a very clubby feel enhanced by the military memorabilia on the walls.

The **H2O** bar in the Ambassador Hotel is a bright, colourful bar with a light-hearted underwater decor theme. If you want just a quiet drink or some meaningful conversation, then go to a bar at a five-star hotel; the bars/pubs elsewhere tend to play very loud music. **Djinns** at the Hyatt is Delhi's eternally popular bar and night club. At the time of writing, **Float** at the Park Royal Hotel was the hip and happening nightspot in Delhi, but given the fickleness of such trends that information may be out of date. **TGIF**, **Blues** and **Pegasus** remain perennially popular bars/pubs with the newer **Daniell's Tavern** appearing to be about to join their ranks. Local newspapers and magazines are the best sources of up-to-date information about which bars are fashionable/happening. **The Gymkhana Club** is a members only club, but if you know someone who is a member, get them to take you there for a drink. It is housed in an old colonial bungalow complete with wooden dance floor, billiard room and library. It's an 'establishment' type of place, but on Thursday evenings, crowds of Delhi's socially prominent young things gather on the lawn for drinks, snacks and dancing (to really loud music).

Coffee houses were popular in Delhi in Shah Jahan's time—men would gather to read poetry, discuss court gossip and smoke hookahs as well as drink coffee there. The coffee bar has recently made a big comeback in Delhi with the very modern Barista leading the way. In seemingly no time, **Barista** outlets have sprung up all over the city, and they keep opening (almost every time one goes out a new Barista is sighted). Barista has brought to Delhi the café/coffee culture that has become an integral part of cosmopolitan city life the world over. The *espresso* served at Barista is authentic and the choices plentiful: *cappuccino*, *macchiato*, *caffe mocha*, *caffe latte* (the IT coffee), *affogato*, *iced coffee* and *frozen coffee*. The good folk at Barista will be happy to explain the differences between each style for you (do not be tempted by those awful shots of sickly sweet syrup; the coffee at Barista is good enough to do without this Americanization. Italians would never add such abominations to their coffee). Barista has a selection of *cakes*, *savouries* and *other drinks* as well. Unlike Delhi's earliest coffee houses, Barista is open to both sexes, though poetry and gossip are still encouraged.

The very best drink of all in Delhi is a refreshing ice-cold *nimbu soda* from the lemonwallah diagonally opposite the town hall in **Chandni Chowk**. This is literally a key-in-the-wall place and the lemonwallah sits up on an elevated perch and 'pops' the old-fashioned marble stoppers on the glass bottles before he hands them to his customers. He seems to be in ceaseless motion in the warmer months of the year. Delhi's power supply is extremely irregular in overcrowded Old Delhi, so rather than rely on refrigeration, the lemonwallah keeps his nimbu sodas chilled on a huge slab of ice. (Visiting Old Delhi is always

Fruit juice at Chandni Chowk

thirsty work and I usually have one nimbu soda on my way up the chowk and one more on the way back. On hot summer days I have been known to double that intake.)

■ Wine with Indian food

Delhi's ruling nobles may have had a penchant for drinking wine but this has never spilt over to the population at large. Whisky, beer and gin are the preferred drinks in Delhi. These are not the sort of drinks that work well with food (with the exception of beer in some circumstances). As a rule, drinks are had before dinner in Delhi and dinner is served only when the drinking is over and done with (giving rise to the infamous Delhi dinner hour which is often very late if the company is lively!).

Recently this has begun to change and Delhiites are developing an interest in and a taste for wine. Good quality imported wines are only available in five-star hotels and are very expensive. There is a growing range of Indian wines available and many of these are quite impressive.

To gain the most out of drinking wine it is important to try and match the right wine with the right food.

In general, white wine is considered to be best with Indian food along with some lighter red styles. As a rule, red wines are served at room temperature and white wines are chilled.

Beaujolais—a fresh light red wine that can be had at room

temperature or chilled; good with lightly spiced Indian snacks and masala dosas.

Merlot—a medium-style red wine; good with most Indian food.

Rose—serve this pink wine nicely chilled; a good partner for tangy Goan-influenced cuisine (Grover's makes an excellent, world class Rose).

Chardonnay—a fruity white wine; pair with coconut-based fish and prawn dishes.

Chablis—dry white; a good all-rounder with Indian food.

Sauvignon Blanc—full-bodied white; considered to be the best match for Indian food (Sula produces a very good Sauvignon Blanc).

Riesling—dry white, fruity in taste; works well with milder styles of Indian food such as wazwaan food and tandoori foods.

Cabernet Sauvignon—this full bodied red is good with game dishes (Grover's again makes an excellent La Reserve Cabernet Sauvignon).

Sparkling white wine—good with anything! Serve chilled. (Sula makes a good sparkling white.)

Anything that is very highly spiced and full of chillies is going to knock the flavour out of any wine. If you enjoy this style of food, then stick to beer.

Some local publications with restaurant and bar listings are *First City*, *Delhi Times* supplement, *Delhi: City Info*, *Delhi Diary* and *The Delhi City* guide.

DIVA
M-8A Greater Kailash II
(M-block Market)
26215673, 26218522

KASBAH
2 N-Block Market
Greater Kailash I
26223328

LA PIAZZA
Hyatt Regency
Bhikaji Cama Place
26791234
Sunday Brunch
12 p.m.-2.30 p.m.

SAN GIMIGNANO
Hotel Imperial
Janpath
23341234

FAB CAFÉ
1 N-Block Market
Greater Kailash 1
26478559, 26221065

PIZZA PIZZA EXPRESS
Ansal Plaza
Khel Gaon Marg
26254892
11 a.m.-11 p.m.

FLAVOURS OF ITALY
52-C DDA Shopping
Complex

(Opposite Moolchand
Hospital)
24645644
11 a.m.-11 p.m.

NIZAM'S KATHI KABABS
H-5 Plaza Cinema Building
Connaught Place
23713078
11 a.m.-11 p.m.

THE GREAT KABAB
FACTORY
Radisson Hotel
NH 8
26129191
7 p.m.-Midnight
Sunday Lunch
12.30 p.m.-3.30 p.m.

COLONEL'S KABABZ
29/1 Defence Colony Market
24264384
11 a.m.–11.30 p.m.

TRIVENI
205 Tansen Marg
10 a.m.-6.30 p.m.

GANGA DHABA
Jawaharlal Nehru University
11 a.m.-11 p.m.

PARIKRAMA
Antriksh Bhavan
22 Kasturba Gandhi Marg
23721616

NIRULA'S
L-Block, Connaught Place
23316694
10.30 a.m.-11 p.m.
Branches all over Delhi
including:
Defence Colony
East of Kailash
GK I
Lajpat Nagar

GOURMET ICES
E-556 Greater Kailash II
26232233
10 a.m.-11 p.m.

THE BIG CHILL
F-32 East of Kailash
26481020

H20
The Ambassador Hotel
Sujan Singh Park
Cornwallis Road
24632600
Noon-Midnight

PATIALA PEG
Hotel Imperial
Janpath
23341234
11 a.m.-Midnight

DJINNS
Hyatt Regency
Bhikaji Cama Place

Ring Road
26791234

FLOAT
Park Royal Hotel
Nehru Place
26223344

TGIF
62 Basant Lok
Vasant Vihar
(Priya Cinema Complex)
26513336

BLUES
N-18 Connaught Place
3310957

PEGASUS BAR
Nirula's Hotel
L-Block Connuaght Place
23322149
11 a.m.-Midnight

DANIELL'S TAVERN
Hotel Imperial
Janpath
23341234
12.30 p.m.-11.45 p.m.

BARISTA
10 a.m.-10 p.m.
Branch all over Delhi including:
Community Centre
Connaught Place
Defence Colony Market
GK I Market

Khan Market
New Friends Colony
Saket Cinema Complex
South Extension II
Priya Cinema Complex,
Vasant Vihar

D.T. Vedprakash
Lemonwallah
Chandni Chowk
(Diagonally opposite
Town Hall)

BIBLIOGRAPHY

■ General

Achaya, K.T., *Indian Food: A Historical Companion* (New Delhi: Oxford University Press, 1994)

Achaya, K.T., *A Historical Dictionary of Indian Food* (New Delhi: Oxford University Press, 1998)

Ali, A., *Twilight in Delhi: A Novel* (New York: New Directions, 1940)

Dalrymple, W., *City of Djinns: A Year in Delhi* (London: HarperCollins, 1993)

Eraly, A., *The Gem in the Lotus* (New Delhi: Penguin Books, 2000)

Frykenberg, R.E., *Delhi Through the Ages: Essays in Urban History, Culture and Society* (New Delhi: Oxford University Press, 1986)

Gupta, N., *Delhi Between Two Empires 1803–1931: Society, Government and Urban Growth* (New Delhi: Oxford University Press, 1981)

Jhabvala, C.S.H., *Delhi: Stones and Streets* (New Delhi: Ravi Dayal, 1990)

Kaul, H.R., *Historic Delhi* (New Delhi: Oxford University Press, 1985)

Narain, P., *The Essential Delhi Cookbook* (New Delhi: Penguin Books, 2000)

Singh, K., *Delhi: A Novel* (New Delhi: Penguin Books, 1990)

Singh, K., ed., *City Improbable: Writings on Delhi* (New Delhi: Penguin Books, 2001)

Singh, P., *Of Dreams and Demons: An Indian Memoir* (London: Gerald Duckworth & Co, 1994)

Thapar, R., *A History of India*, vol. I (New Delhi: Penguin Books, 1966)

◼ Ancient Delhi

Auboyer, J., *Daily Life in Ancient India* (London: Morrison Limited, 1961)

Mani, B.R., *Delhi: The Threshold of the Orient (Studies in Archaeological Evidence)* (New Delhi: Aria Books, 1997)

Parkas, O., *Food and Drink in Ancient India* (New Delhi: Munshi Ram Manohar Lal, 1961)

Puri, B.N., *India as Described by Early Greek Writers* (New Delhi: Delhi Indological Book House, 1971)

Singh, U., *Ancient Delhi* (New Delhi: Oxford University Press, 1999)

Singh, V.B., *Social Life in Ancient India* (New Delhi: Light & Life Publishers, 1981)

◼ Sultanate Delhi

Jackson, P., *The Delhi Sultanate* (London: Cambridge University Press, 1999)

Gibb, H.A.R., trans., *The Travels of Ibn Battuta*, vol. III (London: Cambridge University Press, 1971)

■ Mughal Delhi

Ansai, A., *Social Life of the Mughal Emperors* (New Delhi: Shanker Printers, 1994)

Bernier, F., *Travels in the Mughal Empire* (London: Oxford University Press, 1916)

Blake, S., *Shahjahanabad: The Sovereign City in Mughal India* (London: Cambridge University Press, 1991)

Gascoigne, B., *The Great Mughals* (New Delhi: B-1 Publications, 1971)

■ British Delhi

Jones, M.B., *The Viceroys of India* (London: Constable, 1982)

Wise, M., ed., *True Tales of British India* (London: In Print Publishing, 1993)

Evans, H., *Looking Back on India* (London: Frank Cass, 1988)

Achaya, K.T., *The Food Industries of British India* (New Delhi: Oxford University Press, 1994)

Ghose, I., ed., *Memsahibs Abroad* (New Delhi: Oxford University Press, 1996)

Edwardes, M., *The Sahib and the Lotus* (London: Constable, 1988)